T0064497

The
BASEBALL
BIBLE

The
BASEBALL
BIBLE

HOW TO PLAY THIS GAME

Lenzy Kelley Jr.

authorHOUSE®

AuthorHouse™
1663 Liberty Drive
Bloomington, IN 47403
www.authorhouse.com
Phone: 1 (800) 839-8640

Published by AuthorHouse   08/07/2015

ISBN: 978-1-5049-2662-1 (sc)
ISBN: 978-1-5049-2661-4 (e)

Print information available on the last page.

CONTENTS

PREFACE

The genesis of this book is this author's view point on how the game should be played. Some of the baseball theory cited in this book comes from views stated by News casters and radio and TV sports analysis. However if anyone strongly disagrees with points in this book, feel free to contact me at Lenzyk@yahoo.com. If I concur with your assessment, I'll then make a change to be cited in my 2nd edition. Also, because of baseballs evolving rule changes, there may be new rules or policy changes not incorporated in this book.

Chapter 1

INTRODUCTION

Baseball may have lost its title of American's favorite past time, however thousands of kids across the globe play and enjoy this game. From those thousands only 750 evolve to become good enough to play at the major league level. Out of the 750, perhaps 1/10 will have unique outstanding talent. Because of the global expansion of baseball, we now have players and star players from Japan, Taiwan, Korea, Latin American, Mexico, South America and now Cuba (With improved relations between America and Cuba). Like thousands of other kids across the globe, this author has always dreamed of being a professional baseball player. My favorite team was the Brooklyn Dodgers. Those days growing up in New York City were exciting times for baseball fans as there were 3 major league teams (Dodges, NY Giants and NY Yankees). Unfortunately, I still remember the morning I read the news paper and discovered that the Dodgers had left town and moved to LA. That one event broke my heart because as a child I had never known hurt or disappointment before. Later as I grew older I discovered like thousands of other kids that I was not good enough to play professional baseball. However, I remained a fan.

BASE RUNNING

If the outfielder does not charge the ball, the runner should try for an extra base.

If you hit a ball Into the gap and the outfielder misplays it, with two outs you should try for 3rd base.

If you're trying to determine if you should try for 3rd, don't look at the outfielders, look at the 3rd base coach

When a line drive is hit, the runners should freeze and not cross over to far until they see if the ball is caught or went through for a hit.

On a fly ball to right field, the runner on second should go 1/3 of the way to third base not half. That will enable him to get back to 2nd base, tag up and go to third base if the ball is hit deep enough.

If you're sure the ball is going to be caught, you should tag up.

A runner is on first base, the ball is hit slowly to the second baseman who decides to tag the runner then throw to first base for the double play. The runner should back track towards first base to avoid the tag. Thus, giving the runner time to reach first base to avoid the double play. If the second baseman throws to the short stop who coving second base, it will still be too late to complete the double play.

Getting to third base is important. Once you reach third you don't need a hit to score. You can score on a balk, wild pitch or error

The best way to survive a run down on the base path is to try and get interference called against the defensive player. The defensive player cannot make contact with the runner without the ball.

If the catcher blocks the outside of the plate, the runner must be able to hook slide to nick the unblocked inside portion of the plate.

On a base hit with a runner on second base, the batter may intentionally try to get caught in a run down if the runner is slow and needs more time to cross home plate.

The runner on second base must watch the ball if it's in front on him to avoid being thrown out at third base.

With a comeback towards the pitcher's mound, the runner on second should wait or freeze to determine if the ball is over the pitcher's head before trying to reach third. If the pitcher gloves the ball, the runner gets caught in a run down

If the pitcher is covering home the runner on third base must put pressure on the pitcher by coming home.

Head first slides can cause injuries to fingers, hands and shoulders.

Rounding third base a runner should not stop or hesitate. Doing so could cause an injury. Follow instructions from the third base coach

A runner may tag up and go half way down the line but if he sees the throw is good he should turn around and go back.

When stealing, you don't want to make the first or third out at third base.

Runner on first with a ball hit to the second baseman, the runner should peak, hesitate or stop to see where ball is and to make sure the ground ball is caught or goes through before running, to avoid being hit by the ball.

With a runner on second, if the ball is hit to the short stop, and the runner see's the ball, he should not try for third. However, if the ball is hit slowly the runner should be ab le to reach third without being thrown out.

Tall pitchers with high leg kicks are easier to run on.

Base runners should watch the trajectory of the ball. If the throw is low, it's possible that the catcher may not come up with it cleanly. Thus, allowing the runners to advance.

Sliding into first base is dangerous, and not a sound play. A head first slide requires you to slow down. By standing up, most likely you would have been safe anyway.

On a squeeze play, the runner on third must wait until the pitcher has committed to the play before dashing for home. The batter also has to successfully bunt the ball.

If given to you, take second base to stay out of the double play.

You have to run on curves, change-up and breaking balls (soft pitches).

If the hitter strikes out and the ball gets away from the catcher, the Hitter should run to first base. The catcher could throw the ball wildly to first. Do not stand around and wait to be tagged out. Make the catcher put the ball in play.

Do not make the third out by getting picked off of second base by the pitcher or catcher.

If the runner makes a wide turn at first and the outfielder throws behind him to first, if the ball gets to first ahead of him, he should dive back to the first base bag with his right hand extended then pull it back and try to hook the bag with his left hand.

The runner on third can tag and take off for home if the fly ball to right field causes the right fielders momentum to carry him away from the play or a throw to home.

With a runner on second, on a hit to right field with two outs, you make the outfielder throw you out. If the catcher comes up the first base line, the runner can hook the left side of the plate.

Base runner on first should run all out to second on a hit in the event the outfielder bobbles the ball he can continue to third.

Runner on second should be careful as to not rope trail the runner into an out by faking a steal to third. Run or stay put as you may disturb the batter as the runner on second is part of the background.

Runner should go from first to third with one out. Make the outfielder throw you out.

Base runners should be alert for balls in the dirt and be prepared to advance.

A lot of runner's are thrown out at home plate because they can only slide with one leg.

If the runner reads the throw after tagging up, he can still stop and go back. However, if he puts his head down he can't see or read the throw and may get thrown out.

Do your home work and know the arm strength of the opposition's outfield.

Just because the opposition's outfielder's have strong throwing arms, they may not be accurate. If the outfielder's make strong but inaccurate throws, you can still tag up and advance or score.

Base runners should also know the efficiency of the opposition's outfielder's and infielders. The outfielders may have weak arms but do a good job in hitting the cut-off man. The throw from the infielder to home will be more accurate in cutting down a runner.

With the infield in, you can't run on contact.

Back end runners must make sure the front end runner goes before you do.

Runner on 3rd base should be even with the 3rd BM in the event the ball is hit directly to third.

For a ball in the dirt, there's no requirement for the tail runner to break for 2nd just because the front runner breaks for 3rd.

Runner on 3rd should go as far as the 3rd BM down the line. For a come back to the pitcher, he will look the runner back to 3rd. However, if the runner is front of the 3rd BM, he could be picked off.

Runners rounding 3rd base should remember that there is a loop rounding 3rd before you can start the straight line to home plate.

1-2 count is a good count to run on as the hitter is thinking FB but the pitcher may attempt to cross him up with an off speed pitch.

2-0 is also a good pitch count to run on as the pitcher won't pitch out

Low split finger pitches are also good pitches to run on as the catcher may have problems with the low pitch.

With runners on 1st and 3rd with one out, a ball is hit on the ground; the runner on 3rd must run to home plate to score before the double play is turned.

If a pitcher is struggling, don't help him out by running yourself out of an inning with bad base running. (i.e., stealing a base, stretching single to double or being thrown out at home plate.

When stealing do not come off of the bag as the glove tag is still on you.

A high leg kick is a good base stealing situation.

When attempting to steal 2nd or 3rd, it's important not to start your slide too late. If you slide too late, the momentum of the slide will possibly cause your ankle to twist beneath you as you slide over the bag.

If the catcher is blocking the plate, you must run him over.

If the catcher is not blocking the plate, then slide.

If the catcher comes up the 3rd base line blocking the path to home plate, you must run him over.

It should be noted that catchers can no longer block the plate.

When running from home to 1st, the runner must be in foul territory. If the runner is running on the grass, the umpire will call interference and the runner is called out.

With a runner on second and the batter hits a base hit to the outfield, on a play at the plate the hitter should take 2nd base.

When ball is hit deep to center, if momentum takes the center-fielder to the wall with his back turned towards home plate, the runners should tag and move up.

With two outs, the runner on 1st should try to steal 2nd base.

Runner on 3rd base should lead off the bag in foul territory. If in fair territory and is hit by the ball, he is out.

Runners should slide to the outside of the bag during a steal attempt.

On base hit to left field, the runner should take a wide turn in the event the left fielder bobbles the ball. Also, it's unlikely that the left-fielder will throw out the runner on 1st base making the turn.

Runner should not turn to look at other runners as it slows you down. Take your instructions from the 3rd base coach.

In an effort to break up a double play, if you try to take out the 2nd baseman, you must stay in the base line and slide in front of the bag. If you slide behind 2nd base it not legal and you may be called out by the umpire.

With a runner on 1st base and on a fair ball that hits home plate, the hitter should run to 1st base. If he doesn't run, the catcher can then tag him out at the plate and throw to second to get the runner from 1st base. If the hitter had ran, the play to 2nd would have been a force play and the relay to 1st may not have resulted in a double play.

Do not attempt a steal of 2nd base with two outs and a 2-2 count. The hitter may swing to protect the runner. If the count goes 3-2, the runner will then be running.

Base runners should remember to run hard at all times. All it takes is one bobble and you're on.

Down 3-0, there's no reason to try and stretch a single into a double unless you can make it standing up.

The runner on third wants the outfielder to think he's going and to make an aggressive throw thus possibly causing an error.

With runners on 1st and 3rd with two outs, if the runner on 1st attempts to steal 2nd, and he sees that he's going to be thrown out, he should stay in a rundown long enough for the runner on 3rd to score.

When running to 1st base, unless you're planning on stretching a single, you must turn to your right. Otherwise if you turn left and are off the bag, you can get tagged out.

Run on contact plays will run you right out of an inning. With a runner on 3rd if the ball is hit directly at any infielder, unless it's a high chop, the runner will be thrown out at the plate.

Base runners should watch the trajectory of the ball as it leaves the pitchers hand. If it's in the dirt, the runner should take off for the next base.

On a possible double play ball, the runner on 1st should not go into 2nd base standing up. He should slide and attempt to break up the double play.

A slow runner on 3rd should not run on contact. He should wait to see if the ball goes through

Runners should not attempt to steal while the pitcher is standing on the mound with the ball in his hand.

The 3-1 count is a good count to run on. It keeps you out of the DP as the batter most likely will get a good pitch to hit.

With a head first slide into 2nd base, runners should tuck in or pull their right arm to avoid the swipe tag.

If you swing and miss at a 3rd strike and the ball gets away from the catcher, do not stand at home and wait for the catcher to retrieve the ball and tag you out. Run to first base and make the catcher put the ball in play. He could throw it away thus allowing you to take 2nd and then score on a base hit.

With the shift on, the base runner on 2nd should be careful not to be doubled up or caught in a run down as the SS or 2nd BM may be playing closer to 2nd base.

Chapter 3

BUNTING

If a hitter squares around to bunt then pulls the bat back, he may fool the pitcher into throwing a fastball down the middle of the plate.

Show bunt, pull back and swing away if infielders come in too fast.

During a bunt or sacrifice if the pitcher is wild, wait for him to throw a strike. Don't help him out by going after a pitch out of the strike zone.

When bunting the hitter must get the ball pass the pitcher between the pitcher and 1st or the pitcher and 3rd.

When bunting you don't want to make the first or third out at third base.

During a sacrifice the hitter does not want to bunt the ball directly to the 3rd baseman or 1st baseman. If the ball is bunted too sharply, there could be a force play at second or third.

Bunts can loosen an infield up. The next time the batter comes up, the infield may be a step closer.

One key to a successful bunt is not commit or give your intentions too soon.

The hitter can show bunt to move the infield around.

When bunting, the bat head must be out in front of the plate not behind.

The bat head will deaden the ball.

You have to bunt strikes. Put the bat at the top of the SZ and don't ludge.

When bunting, if the infielders are up real close, the batter could chop down on the ball. The ball may go over the heads of the infielders or stay in the air long enough for the runners to advance.

In a bunt situation, the batter may not be a good bunter. However, he must get the head out in front in fair territory.

To bunt successfully, square around put the barrow of the bat at top of the strike zone then go down.

On a bunt down the third base line, the catcher should bare hand the ball, turn to his left, pivot on right foot to get something on the throw to first. Turning and pivoting to his left will give him momentum and power in his throw. If he turns right there will be no power in his throw.

Fake bunt on first pitch, pitcher may then throw fastball down the middle.

Fake bunt also has infielder's moving around crating holes.

A high fast ball is the hardest pitch to bunt against.

If you show bunt too soon, the third baseman could creep up closer.

Show bunt to draw infield in then try to hit through drawn in infield.

First and third is a good bunt situation. You can get a runner home and move runner to second base. The batter should bunt the ball to the right side beyond the pitcher and make the second baseman field the ball.

Runners with speed will bring the infielder's in closer.

In a bunt attempt, push the ball towards the 1st BM or 3rd BM in front of the pitcher. Have the ball dissect the 1st BM and the pitcher or the 3rd BM and the pitcher.

To bunt, rotate your body, get barrel of bat in front of home plate. Also, move knees to get the bat up and down not your hands

When squaring around to bunt do not wrap your top hand around the bat. The hitter could sustain an injury to his hand.

Drag bunt is a misnomer. You must be standing still to lay down a good bunt. If you're moving, it's hard to get the bat down. If the pitcher has high velocity, it's hard to deaden the ball.

Everyone should practice bunting in the event you come to the plate in an obvious bunt situation. If you are a bad bunter, now the manager has to make a decision whether to leave you in or pitch hit with another player with better bunting skills.

CATCHERS

An ideal catcher must be athletic, a good defender, durable, can draw walks and has power. In addition, the catcher must have the ability to analyze detailed reports formulated from the team scouts in preparation of the game plan for his team's pitchers to use in attacking the opposing teams hitters.

Catchers must back up the first baseman.

During a bunt down the first base line, if the ball is rolling slowly the catcher should wave off the first baseman and throw the ball to the 2nd baseman that should be covering first base. It's an easier play for the catcher as he is going in that direction. Whereas, the first baseman would have to field the ball, turn around then throw.

During a run down between 1st and 2nd, once again the catcher must back up the 1st baseman in the event he misses the tag during the run down.

If a pitch is close or near the plate corner, the catcher should frame it for the umpire.

If a batter makes an adjustment by not pulling and driving the ball, the catcher can also make an adjustment by calling pitches inside on the hands.

Catchers should not stab at pitches on the corner. Rather they should frame then smoothly and move so as to influence the umpire. They should present close pitches around the strike zone as strikes and not present strikes as balls. (Sell border line pitches to the umpire as strikes)

The catcher should present a stable target to the pitcher by not moving the glove hand around.

To throw a runner out attempting to steal, the catcher must receive the ball in a good position then make an accurate throw.

To avoid possible injuries, catchers on pop-up behind the plate must watch out for bats, helmets and other debris left around the on deck circle.

On a pop up in front of home plate, the catcher should take charge. The catcher should go out and come back towards the ball facing home plate. His back should not be facing home plate.

If the catcher sets up too soon with a runner on second base, the runner can see where the catcher is leaning and determine where the pitch is to be thrown and relay that info to the hitter.

If a catcher is set up on the inside of the plate, he is not expecting a curve ball.

If the catcher widens his stance too soon, he sends a message to the hitter that an off-speed pitch is coming.

If the catcher shifts too soon, he may give away the pitch location. Some catchers play tricks by moving and allowing the batter to peek then at the last second shift again.

The catcher must be careful as not to break a pitchers rhythm by going to the mound.

Fastball away gives the catcher a better chance at throwing out the runner attempting to steal second base.

For a ball in the dirt, to avoid an injury the catcher should put his bare hand behind his back and block the ball with his chest.

For balls in the dirt, a catcher can also shift his body to get in front of the ball, knock it down, smother it, and not try to back hand it.

The catcher must get on top of the plate to make sure the runner does not score. Make runner go around, catch the ball, block the plate and make the tag.

Collisions at home can cause injuries. If the catcher receives the ball early enough, he could then try the sweep and tag. However, the ball could be knocked out of the mitt.

A throw to the catcher from the right fielder or right side of the infield is difficult for catchers as they lose sight of the runner coming from third.

If a pitcher has good control, the catcher should be set up right on the corner.

Batters can at times sense position of the catcher. Some catchers will set up inside and move outside at the last second. The hitter then thinks the pitch will be inside but it comes outside. So the catcher should set up at the last moment (inside or outside) so the batter can't determine the pitch location

For a pitch in the dirt, the catcher must go down to his knees to smoother or block the ball, not just stabbing at ball with the catcher's mitt.

If a catcher has to lean to his right on a throw from left field, he may not be able to keep this foot planted to block the plate.

If a catcher see's that a throw to the plate won't be in time, he should then move out the way of the runner. This avoids a collision with the runner with the ball getting away thus allowing the runner to advance to second or third.

If a big physical runner is barreling down the third base line towards home, the catcher must decide if he wants to block the plate. In doing so, there will be a collision which may result in an injury. It may be best to move out the way, catch the throw and attempt a swipe tag. By giving the runner some room, he has no reason to run into you as the plate is within sight. However, with a good throw, you can still tag him out and avoid an injury.

On a throw to home, if the catcher is too far from the plate, the runner from third could hook slide to avoid the swipe tag.

If the catcher is too far up the first base line, he can't get back in time to block the plate.

The catcher should keep the ball in front of me him so that the runner can't gage the ball. If the ball bounces to the left or right of the catcher, the runner can see the ball and can then determine if it's far enough away for him to take another base.

With runners on first and third, if the runner on first try's to steal, the catcher should look the runner on third back to the bag then throw to second or not throw at all.

When the third baseman comes in the catcher should then go out to cover third.

It's important for the catcher and pitcher to be on the same frequency to preclude the catcher from being crossed up.

Catchers must square up to pitches in the dirt and try to smother.

If a pitcher is having problems nipping the corners, the catcher may be forced to set up in the middle of the plate. However, in that instance, the pitcher needs a good letter high fastball and sinker since he's now pitching down the middle of the plate.

Some pitchers want their catchers to set up a few inches off the plate so they can hit the spot and the catcher does not have to move the glove to catch it.

For a pop up near the pitcher's mound, the catcher should not rhome near or past the pitcher's mound. He should be called off by one of the infielders.

For a ball in the dirt, the catcher should turn his glove hand the other way and drop down to his knee's to prevent the past ball.

A catcher with a reputation for a good snap throw to 1st is extremely helpful to the pitcher for holding the runners close to the bag.

A catcher who can make strong throws to 2nd base on one knee and make snap throws to 1st base in the squat position is rare and should be the back-up if not the stating catcher.

The catcher should move up to meet throw from outfielders to shorten the throw to 2nd base if needed.

On a pop up down the right field line near 1st base, if the 1st basemen goes out too far the catcher should track/trail the play and go to 1st base in the event:

Ball is dropped and lands in fair territory there's a play at 1st if runner didn't run hard to 1st.

If a runner is at 1st, he could be doubled off if ball is caught and he doesn't get back in time.

If the runner from 3rd attempts to dodge the tag at home plate by dancing around the catcher, the catcher should sit on home plate and let the runner come to him.

If the pitcher is throwing a lot of sliders, the catcher must be good at blocking the plate and digging pitches out of the dirt.

On a throw from the right-fielder, the catcher does not see the runner tagging from 3rd base until he catches the ball then turns to face the runner. Once he faces the runner, he should then square up, plant his feet and prepare for the collision.

If the catcher is set up outside and the pitch is way inside, there could be a communications problem.

Catcher should use glove and chest protector to keep ball in front of him.

Catcher should protect/not expose non-glove hand to prevent injury.

Late in the game with the game on the line and a runner on $2^{nd,}$ do not flash signs to the pitcher. Walk out to the mound to discuss the next pitch. This will preclude the runner on 2nd from stealing the sign.

The catcher and SS should have a signal to alert the SS or 2nd BM that the catcher intends to come up throwing in an attempt to pick off the runner on 2nd base.

With a runner on 1st and 3rd, if the runner is 1st is running, the catcher should look the runner on 3rd back to 3rd before throwing to 2nd.

See below for new plate blocking rules for catchers

Chapter 5

HITTERS

A hitter's job is to find a pitch to hit. To do so, do not guess or look for pitches. Trust yourself. Sit back, let your trust and your hands see the ball and hit the ball. Follow trajectory as it leaves the pitcher's hand. Adjust as appropriate. Be patient, take walks if need be. Stay away from pitches outside of strike zone. Don't swing at pitches in on the hand or at your eye level. Take note of the speed, movement, and break of the ball. Don't wind up and jump out in front. Have a good short compact swing. Try to develop a clean swing with no jerky motions. Dave Winfield had a hitch in his swing. If he had choked up on the bat and shorten his swing, he may have played another 2-3 years. With his size and strength, he was still strong enough to hit the ball out of the park.

Hitter's should do some homework on the pitcher he is to face before the game.

When facing a sinker ball pitcher, hitters must get under the pitch. If not, they will pound it in the ground.

Hitter's should stay in the strike zone.

A change-up gets the bat out in front. The hitter must wait for it.

Good hitter's should take their walks (work into the count) and use the entire field as opposed to being a dead pull hitter.

If you try to pull the folk ball, you will hit a fly ball.

If you try to pull an outside fastball, you will hit a ground ball.

If you tip back your shoulders and get under a pitch, you will pop it up.

Swing through pitch, keep level swing, hands in, square hips, front leg out, stay back on back leg and keep head down. Use hands and wrist to get bat head through the SZ.

Your batting stance should be balanced. You should not be falling away from the plate as you swing. When you fall away, you lose power and are not exerting any punch into your swing.

With a runner on second base and nobody out, the batter's job is to move the runner to third base.

After a four pitch walk, the batter has to be looking for a fast ball down the middle.

On a 2-1 count, a good hitting spot should see a good pitch. The batter can be selective or even take a close pitch.

On 1-2, you have to be more aggressive towards anything near the strike zone.

Hits should be run out. Triples become doubles. Doubles become singles because hitters don't run out their hits.

Batters may want to swing at the first pitch against a sinker ball pitcher as opposed to being down in the count 0-2 then having to look at a sinker.

Hitters should watch the hitter ahead of him to see what the pitcher is throwing that works for him.

3-1 is a good hitter's pitch. The batter should look for his pitch and not over swing, just put good wood on the ball and swing through. 3-1 is also a good hit and run pitch. If the pitcher pitches away, the batter should try to punch the ball to the right side to advance the runner. 3-1 with a good hitter on deck, the batter should get a good pitch to hit.

If a pitcher is wild, make him throw a strike. Don't help him out by swinging at a bad pitch.

If a pitcher walks the bases full, if the manager doesn't take him out the next batter should take until he starts to throw strikes.

If a pitcher known for throwing strikes can't find the plate, be patient. He may want to grove one over the plate just to get a strike.

To add power to your swing, lift leg, keep weight back, load up with arms or hands and drive through.

Leading with front leg, depletes your power.

Bat head up front with hands back.

The more the hands go back, the more the front shoulders sit in.

To hit the inside pitch, lower your elbow in order to get the barrow of the bat around.

After a walk, the pitch will throw strikes so the batter should see hittable pitches.

If a pitcher is pitching with a large lead late in the game, he won't fool around with breaking pitches. He'll be throwing fastballs. As such, the batter should be swinging. No call third strikes.

A hitter's hands should be held above the strike zone. Once you drop them it's hard to get them back up. Hang back and let the hands do the work.

Facing a high knuckle ball pitcher the ball is easier to see and hit. However, there is a tendency to pop up. For that reason most hitters prefer a low knuckle ball pitcher.

If you're facing a new pitcher take a few pitches to observe the delivery, style, speed and type of pitches.

Hitter's have to recognize that pitches come over the strike zone then drop out of the strike zone.

Left handed hitters must fight off pitches and go to the opposite field in-lieu of trying to pull the ball.

RHH against LHP should go to right or up the middle and not always try to pull.

Best way to hit a left handed pitcher is to take him the other way.

Hitter's with a wide stance and stride won't be fooled by a pitch. However, the stance is hard on the knees.

Hitter's who watch their home runs upset the pitcher and may make them feel shown-up.

Hitters with high kicks will have timing problems

To generate greater bat speed, use smaller bat with a thinner handle.

Hitters should let pitch come to them and not lunge at pitches. Hitter's body should stay vertical with head in for a level swing.

Hitters must swing through the pitch and not swing flat footed.

Hitter's should keep their heads down when swinging and follow through to the ball.

Do not reach meekly at pitches, adjust to the strike zone. Shorten swing and make contact.

If the pitcher has a good breaking pitch and a good hard fastball, if the hitter is guessing, he could be too early on the BP or too late on the FB.

If you're guessing, you could just wait for your pitch but you run the risk of being called put on strikes.

Hitters should be at the video to reinforce the positive. Don't wait for a slump.

Batters should follow the ball from the pitchers arm slot, or pick up the ball from behind the head up top or on the side, then see the ball - hit the ball.

Early in the count, the batter has a better chance of handling the inside pitch. At 0-2, the batter becomes more defensive.

Eight place batters should get good pitches to hit. (In the National League) ?

LHH should back off the plate a little to get a better look at RHP slider.

LHH facing a sinker ball pitcher has to think going up the middle or the opposite field as the sinker will trail out over the plate. Otherwise, he'll hit a ground ball.

The sinker is harder to hit for a RHH as the pitch trails in.

Hitters in general should back off of plate to give a better view of all pitches and to enable hitter to better handle the inside pitch.

Sometimes for a 220 hitter, his best chance to get a hit is the first pitch fastball down the middle from the pitcher.

Hitter's down in the batting order may not get any respect from pitchers. As such, they may see fast balls grooved down the middle.

When a pitcher is up 0-2, he basically has 2 pitches to expand the zone. Do not help him out by going after a play out of the strike zone. Make him make a quality pitch.

With runners on base at 0-2, the hitter must find a way to put the ball in play.

0-2, hitter should go into defensive mode and keep ball in play.

Good hitter's will spray the ball around by hitting where the ball is pitched as opposed to trying to pull the ball.

If you anticipate a fast ball, you must get the bat head out early.

When facing a submarine pitcher, hitter's should watch the ball, not the pitcher.

Hitter's who do well against LH starting pitchers for some reason do not do well against LH specialty reliever's.

With a runner on second with no outs, you must move the runner to third via a bunt or hitting the ball to the right side of the infield.

Hitters with speed should get on top of pitch, hit it into the ground and beat it out.

For a fast ball down, drop bat down on the pitch.

Against hard throwing pitcher's, the hitter does not have to swing hard. The pitcher is doing most of the work. Just swing to make contact.

If you hit with a wide stance, you will need upper body strength to hit from the waist up.

If a hitter is in a slump, he should start thinking up the middle or going to the opposite field.

If the pitcher is wild, he may be forced to come down the middle of the plate.

Hitter's with an open stance will have problems reaching pitches on the outside of the plate.

To hit to the opposite field, let the pitch come in deep into the strike zone then swing late at the late moment.

For down and in pitches, pull back elbows and drive to the right side.

If you have a hitch in your swing, it will take longer to get your bat through the strike zone.

Some hitters have a leg kick in their swing. Eliminate the kick and you can then wait and see the pitch better and handle the breaking pitches better.

For a LHH facing a LHP, the hitter should move closer to the plate, keep right shoulder in to enable reach to outside of the plate. Reach for outside pitch and shoot the other way.

LHH should slap ball to left side of the infield (i.e. Baltimore Chopper)

A hitter need good knee's to hit sinker as you must go down to dig it up.

If a hitter does not drive a runner in he has to make a productive out. That is a ground ball or sacrifice fly to get a run home and move runners up.

To hit a sinker you have to swing to miss under it to catch it when it does sink. Otherwise, you top it into the ground

Hitters have to be patient with sinker ball pitchers. Consider going up the middle or to the opposite field.

To hit a knuckle ball, if high let it fly. If low, let it go.

You can hit a 99-100 mph pitch if thrown below the belt. However, it's difficult to hit above the belt.

Try to extend a pitcher into an 8-10 pitch count to give your team mates an opportunity to see his repertoire

If a pitcher won't pitch inside, then lean over the plate to reach the outside corner but beware of the brush back pitch.

To hit a curve, you have to pick up the rotation.

Hit sinkers to the opposite field.

When facing a hard throwing pitcher, you don't have to swing hard. Just shorten your swing and speed up the bat head speed.

Smart hitter's do try and gage arm speed.

For hitter's with patience who walk a lot, eventually pitchers will begin to throw hittable pitches, most likely fastballs. Go deep into the count and hit to the opposite field. Don't try to pull the ball.

High fastballs above the waist are hard to hit. The results are strike outs and pop up's.

Hitter's falling away cannot hit the outside pitch.

Down and in is a good pitch for a LHH.

LHH can also wait a little longer and take the pitch to left center field.

When a LHH pulls a sinker ball, he will hit a ground ball to 2nd base. Go with the pitch and hit to the opposite field.

If you're the type of hitter that like's to guess, if the catcher is on the outside of the plate, the pitch most likely will be outside.

If the pitcher can hit the inside corner, for the batter to hit it with the front barrow of the bat, he will hit it foul.

A RHH facing LHP with runner on second and LHH due up. Hitter should not worry about hitting to the right side of the infield, just attempt to drive the runner in.

If the pitcher is throwing first pitch strikes, then the next time around in the batting order, the hitter should start swinging at the first pitch.

If hitter is trying to pull the ball, he may have to commit his swing early to get the bat head out in front.

Do not inside out a pull ball.

If you're the lead-off hitter and the pitcher was just up, take a few pitches to give the pitcher a chance to rest.

Hitters have to be able to handle the hard fastball straight down the middle of the plate.

Even if you're jammed, keep your swing level.

Bring hands in close to body, up front with elbows inside the pitch. Throw shoulder back towards the pitcher. When jammed force pitch to opposite field.

Cut down on big swing and drive pitch to right field. Keep shoulders back, bat level and don't collapse the elbows.

When the bases are loaded, the pitcher is in a jam. Hitter should look out over the plate as the pitcher does not want to miss inside and put pitch over the plate.

When the infield shift is put on, don't help out the opposing team by trying to pull the ball. Try and hit to the opposite field. By pulling the ball you are hitting into the teeth of the defense set up against you.

Hitters who hit for average mostly keep their bats in the zone longer with a level swing. (Not for power) as opposed to hitters with a loop in their swing. The bat is not in the zone as long.

Good hitters will handle away pitches and react well to inside pitches.

The longer a batter battles a pitcher; the better the chances to get a hit as he has seen most of the pitchers pitches'. In addition, the pitcher is prone to give in and give the hitter something he can hit.

Facing a hard thrower, you swing quicker not harder. You swing quicker by using your hands not your body (Hank Aaron and Ernie Banks used their hands and wrist).

When the pitcher is throwing hard, do not swing hard, just get bat in hitting zone as quickly as possible. Don't try to pull, just make contact.

For a pitch out and up, the hitter should swing level and go to the opposite field.

To drive a runner home from 3rd, drive the ball up the middle. Even if a play is made or the ball is knocked down, the runner should score. If the ball is hit sharply to the left or right side of the infield, there could be a play at the plate.

To get great extension, keep head down, bat head down, pull hands in and top hand loose.

For a pitch out over the plate, swing through it without trying to pull it.

Tailing hard sinking FB is hard to hit as opposed to a running FB over the plate.

With a 0-2 count, the hitter should cut down on his swing and see the ball as long as possible. Just put good wood on ball and put in play.

When hitter's over stride or has a long stride, he loses power as the bat slows and the hips lock. The hitter cannot rotate or turn his hips.

When pitchers fall behind in count, they must now hit more of the plate.

If a pitcher has a true fast ball with no movement, the hitter does not have to adjust.

The runner on 2nd base must be moved to 3rd. A lead-off double cannot be wasted.

It's hard for a hitter to get on top of a good hard FB

If hitters go to the opposite field, the pitcher may be forced to throw fast balls.

The batter must ask umpire for time out before stepping out of the batter's box.

If in a slump, shorten swing and choke up on the bat.

After pitcher throws to first base, the hitter can look for the change up.

Pull hands in to inside out the pitch to the opposite field.

Don't chase FB up above the letters, it's hard to get on top of to hit.

With a big lead, hitters on the losing end should see more FBs.

With LHP pounding inside with FBs, the RHH must quickly get the bat out in front in order to pull the ball.

LHP throwing FBs inside to LHH, if hitter is late, he will pop up.

When hitters are jammed they will hit weak infield grounders or pop up.

Power pitchers will sometimes hang breaking pitches

The hitter should step out of the box (call time out first) when a pitcher is in a rhythm and working fast.

Hitter should not help the pitcher who is trying to expand the strike zone.

Lenzy Kelley Jr.

Hitters with an open stance can see the ball with both eyes better than a hitter with a closed stance.

If 1st batter makes an out with the first pitch, the 2nd batter should take the 1st or maybe the 2nd pitch also. You don't want the pitcher to have a 1-2-3 inning having retired the side with a minimum of pitches.

Hitters must quickly recognize the pitch once it leaves the pitchers hand and track it into the hitting zone.

If the pitcher is pitching away from the hitters strength (dead pull hitter), the hitter should go with the pitch, and hit to the opposite field.

If the hitter has a long at bat 10-13 pitches (with foul off's), this provides the hitter an opportunity to see the pitchers entire repertoire of pitches and to notice if there is a pattern or sequence for certain pitches.

For a high FB, get the hands above the ball and hit squarely.

If you've never seen a pitcher before check out the arm angle and watch the ball.

Hitter's with a closed stance will have problems with the inside pitch.

If a hit and run is called, the hitter must swing even if the pitch is out of the strike zone.

Hitters should not allow pitchers who work fast to get into a groove. Don't let them get into a comfortable groove thereby making you uncomfortable at the plate. Call time and step out of the box to interrupt the pitchers rhythm

If as a hitter you can't handle the FB, then you cheat. When you cheat you then can't handle the breaking ball.

3-0 and 2-0 area good hitting counts (sit on FB). However, if the pitcher can't find the plate, don't help him out.

To pull a pitch, you must quickly get your hands and the bat head out in front of the pitch. If you hit late, the ball goes to center field or the opposite field.

With a hard throwing FB pitcher, hitters won't get the bat head out ahead quick enough. As such, if contact is made, it will be late with the pitch well over the plate. The batter will hit the ball to center or RF (RHH) to left field (LHH). Outfielders should shade towards right for a RHH and towards left for a LHH.

A RHH hitting against a pitcher who throws sliders can guess slider on the outside corner away.

A LHH should not see sliders from a RHP. He should see FBs away.

If a hitter is not a good two strike hitter, most likely he won't hit for average.

Hitters who have lost their lineup protection must become more discipline without becoming passive as pitchers will make mistakes that you must be prepared to take advantage of.

The best hitters who are often times pitched around or see one hittable pitch every game or two still manage to put up good numbers by being patient

Patience requires that you create a tiny zone you're willing to swing at and be ready to pounce

Hitters can zero in on a spot when they are ahead in the count. If he doesn't get his pitch he can take the walk. Thus building his on base percentage, extend innings and extend the pitchers pitch count. Extending the pitchers pitch count can get your team into the opposing team's bullpen.

In a slump, choke up on the bat, cut down on your swing and try going to the opposite field or up the middle.

In a slump, don't over compensate by taking too many swings in the batting cage.

Hitters must fight off the inside fast ball to keep the pitcher from nipping the inside corner.

If you are a guess hitter, you can cheat and start your swing a little early/sooner and hope for a FB.

Timing is important. If you get the bat head out too soon, you will hook the pitch foul

Hitters should maintain bat speed throughout the strike zone.

Hitters who hold the bat low are better able to handle the inside FB

Hitters must be quick to move their hands to avoid injury from tight inside pitches.

Hitters at bat with the bases loaded and nobody out should recognize that the pressure is on the pitcher. Don't try to do too much.

Hitters should lay off of low sliders (dirt balls). The pitch will most likely will be a ball.

Hitters who sit on and plant their back leg will not generate any power.

A RHH can observe if the runner is going and lay off the pitch

If the pitch is up and away, don't try to pull it, go with the pitch to the opposite field. Just make good contact and take the single. If not, pitchers will continue to attack you until you make the adjustment.

Hitters with a hitch in their swing or who wrap their wrists before swinging will have problems. Both will cause timing problems. Hitters will load up when they see a fat juicy pitch and try to hit a home run. In both cases you won't be able to catch up with the FB. If you can't hit the FB, you're dead meat.

Some hitters put un-do pressure on themselves and try to do too much. That's when the game becomes difficult. The less thinking you do the easier the game becomes.

Big, tall strong hitters should not get caught up into trying to hit home runs. Under normal circumstances, it's hard for big hitters to be good hitters. Because you are big and long you present a bigger strike zone. Concentrate on being a good RBI guy and hit for average.

Statistically, one out of 10 fly balls are hits, 2-3 out of 10 ground balls are hits, and seven out of 10 line drives are hits. Use a level swing and use the whole field.

In case of a shift, learn to use the whole field. That way, you will be able to hit the ball any- where. Do not try to beat the shift. Learn to hit to the opposite field and inside out the pitch.

Things to watch for that will help hitters identify a pitch:

- **Speed**
- **Movement** - the general direction the ball is moving
- **Break** - a sudden shift in direction
- **Ball rotation**
- **Point of release and grip**

If in a slump, take what is given. Bunt, inside out pitches, go to the opposite field and especially take advantage of the vacant infield available during a shift.

Chapter 6

INFIELDERS

Infielders should bend their knees and get their butts down for ground balls.

The first baseman must get down low to follow the track or path of the ball on a short hop.

The first baseman should put weight on left foot so that he can spin into the runner if the runner hits the glove.

With a speed runner at bat who hits a ground ball, infielders should not tap their gloves as it gives the runner an extra step.

The first baseman should be careful as to not range too far from first base, thus taking him out of the play. Let the second baseman field the ball wide of first thereby, leaving the first baseman to cover first. With the first baseman out of the play, the pitcher has to cover first. A fast runner will beat the throw.

If a runner is picked of 1 st base and runs towards 2nd, the 2nd baseman or short stop should move towards 1 st base to help contain the runner.

On a DP ball hit close to the third base bag, the third baseman can use the third base bag to drive off on the throw to first.

Late innings, the first and third baseman should be on the line pushing play to the fat part of the infield not giving up the extra base hit. This forces a team to beat you with 3 singles instead of a double and a single

Cut-off man should quickly pivot, turn and throw to catcher.

With a 5 run lead late in the game, with a left handed batter up, the first baseman should not be holding the runner on.

With a runner on second base and a ball hit up the middle, the short stop or second baseman must dive to knock the ball down and keep the ball in front of them to prevent the runner from scoring

With a runner on second base and a ball is hit to the second baseman, if the second baseman goes to third he has to get the runner otherwise it will be runners on first and third.

When an infielder bare hands a ball he has to transfer the grip to two fingers so that the ball won't sail and he can control the throw.

The second baseman must get back to second base if the right fielder throws to third. This will discourage the runner on first from trying to move to second base.

Second basemen and short stop cannot expect perfect throws for double plays. They must be prepared to make the proper footwork adjustments.

The second baseman should have a shortstop arm.

The third baseman or short stop may short hop the throw to first to get it there faster if the runner is fast and he has a good defensive first baseman.

Late in the game with the first and third baseman guarding the line, you protect against the extra base hit but you give up the gap between third base and short stop and second and first base.

The first baseman should practice scooping up the short hops to first base from throws deep in the hole from the short stop or third baseman with weak arms.

A RH 1st baseman has an advantage over a LH 1st basemen in that his glove hand is closer to the runner.

When the short stop goes deep in the hole, unless he has a strong accurate arm, he'll need to stop, plant his feet and then throw.

To play short stop not only do you need a strong arm but you also have to be an accurate thrower. The arm motion must be short not long. You can't catch the ball and then swing your arm around the back of your body before releasing it. If the SS has long limbs, its becomes hard to shorten the throwing motion

When a ball is hit up the middle, the second baseman should defer to the short stop that has a better chance of throwing out the runner as he is going towards first base as opposed to the second baseman whose momentum is taking him in the opposite direction.

In turning the double play, the short stop throw to second base should be shoulder high. The second baseman should be in position to throw to first before he catches the ball from the short stop.

For shallow pop fly's, infielders should not try to make the sports hi-lite film but defer to outfielders especially if there is to be a throw after the catch. In addition, the outfielders momentum is carrying him forward as such he's in a better [position to throw as opposed to the infielder who's momentum is carrying him backwards.

Infielder's, instead of bare handing the ball, use glove, transfer and throw.

On an attempted steal of third base, the third basemen should go to the bag, straddle the bag and make the tag.

In a steal attempt, the short stop should quickly swipe at the runner then hold the ball up for the umpire to see in order to influence the call.

On a double play ball hit to the first baseman, if the first baseman tags first then throws to second, if the first baseman is right-handed, he must make a perfect throw to second base over the runner's head. This is a much easier play for a left-handed first baseman.

On a throw home, if the throw is off line, it must then be cut off by one of the infielder's.

Do not take routine pop-ups for granted. Gage the ball properly to catch in the glove webbing. If the ball hits the palm of the glove, you may drop it or it pops out.

If the second baseman and short stop need to talk, they should signal for a timeout to keep the man on second base from advancing to third base.

In turning the double play, it's important to get the first out as the runner may beat the throw to first base.

If you miss-play a ground ball, don't panic as there is still time to recover and throw the runner our. However, if you continue to panic during the recovery effort, you will most likely miss-play the ball again.

With a speed runner on 2nd base, the 2nd baseman must hold the runner close to 2nd to prevent the runner from getting a rolling start to 3rd. With a LHH up, the 3rd baseman is shaded towards 2nd. So for a play at 3rd, the 3rd baseman would have a further distance to run to get back to 3rd base.

Good fielders will look the ball into their glove.

The 3rd BM should catch the ball with the back hand in front of his body not behind then plant his feet and fire to first.

The 2nd BM should be aggressive and charge the ball so when he flips the ball to the SS, the SS will have time for the relay to 1st.

In a close game or late in the game, the 1st BM and 3rd BM should guard the line.

In a run down, you run the play back to the previous base not the next advance base.

Infielders must anticipate the angle of the relay throw from the outfielder.

With runners on 2nd and 3rd with one out, and a two run lead, the infield should play back and concede the run.

With the runner on 2nd base attempting to steal 3rd base, the 3rd baseman should block the bag with his knees then swipe the runner with his glove.

When a ball is hit in the infield by a speedy runner, the infielder cannot load up to throw. He must charge, field and throw in one motion.

With speedy runners on, for a potential double play, infielders must quickly get rid of the ball, no soft throws to 2nd base.

During an attempted steal of 2nd base, the short stop should back up the 2nd basemen in the event the throw from the catcher gets away.

If you bobble a ground ball, don't panic, stay calm and stick with the play. If you hurry the throw, you could compound the bobbled ball by throwing it away.

With a runner on 3rd, the infield in and a ground ball hit, if any of the infielders bobble the ball, the play has to go to 1st to get the sure out.

If a runner is not a threat to steal, then don't hold him on. The 1st BM can then play off the bag to plug the gap between 2nd base and 1st base.

For a DP ball hit to the 3rd BM or SS, if hitter is left handed, the 2nd BM may be playing him to pull so the 3rd BM or SS may need to hesitate to give the 2nd BM time to reach 2nd base.

If the runner on 2nd base is nursing an injury, the 2nd baseman should then play straight away.

With a ball hit to deep SS, if the runner is not fast, then the SS should gather himself, plant and throw as opposed to a jump throw which won't have any zing or velocity to beat the runner.

For a comeback to a pitcher, for the pitchers throw to first, the 2nd basemen should back up the 1st basemen in the event the throw from the pitcher gets away from the 1st basemen.

For a comeback to the pitcher on the 2nd base side of the mound, the 2nd BM will break towards the ball not knowing that the pitcher will field it. In doing so, he is out of position for a force play at 2nd base. The SS who is moving towards 2nd to back up the play may be out of position to accept the throw from the pitcher. A throw to 2nd by the pitcher will mostly result in an errant throw. What the pitcher should have done is take the sure out at 1st base or not field the ball at all. By letting the 2nd BM field it, the DP is in order as the SS is moving towards 2nd.

With the bases loaded and one out, the infield should be played half-way. On a slow bouncer, they can come home. On a sharply hit ball they can then try to turn the double play.

In a run down, always chase the runner back to the base he came from.

The 2nd baseman or shortstop when coving 2nd base for a force out or double play should quickly move away from the bag. Make the play and move away. In a double play the runner may try to take out who ever is covering 2nd base. The take out is not necessary for a force play but some runners nevertheless may still try it. So to avoid a possible injury, quickly move away after making the throw to first base.

For a force play at 2nd base if the ball is hit to the 2nd baseman, the short stop must quickly get to the bag to take the throw in order to beat the runner.

A ball hit to the short stop side of 2nd base is the responsibility of the short stop, not the 2nd basemen.

The 1st and 3rd basemen should understand that when guarding the line against an extra base hit, they have reduced their range

Note to 3rd baseman, with a LH pitcher on the mound and a ball hit back to his right, he must field it with his glove hand (right) then spin to throw to 1st base. If you are too close to him, you will interfere with his throw to 1st. If his arm hits you, you may even cause an injury to his pitching arm.

On a bunt attempt up the 1st base line, the 1st BM must read the pitcher to determine if the pitcher can field the bunt. If he can't then the 1st BM can field the bunt and toss to the pitcher or 2nd BM. If the 1st BM commits, the pitcher may not be able to beat the runner to 1st.

The third BM very rarely plays deeper than the short stop.

When infielders charge the plate during a bunt attempt, their lateral movement is reduced.

If the 3rd BM is playing with an injury, with a runner on 2nd the 2nd BM may have to hold the runner closer than normal.

Whenever the pitcher has to cover 1st base. At the end of the play, one of the infielders should come over to talk to the pitcher to give him an opportunity to compose himself and catch his breath.

With a slow runner on 3rd, the infield should play half way not all the way in.

With a speed runner on 1st and with an infield pop-up, the infielder may consider letting the ball drop and force the speed runner at 2nd thus effectively exchanging runners.

Infielder's, specifically the 1st and 3rd BM should not give up on pop up's in foul territory. Don't assume the ball will land in the seats. Play it all the way in the event the ball drifts back and becomes catchable.

Chapter 7

MANAGERS

Managers should emphasis to players the importance of getting to the park on time to enable stretching, batting practice, infield and outfield practice and other cage work. Some players get to the park too early then sit around playing cards or computer games. This is not conductive to good game day preparation

It's the manager's responsibility to prepare the team to play and win. This is done by practicing the execution of all the little things it takes to win. Things such as pitchers throwing strikes, hitters moving runners along and getting hits with runners in scoring position, outfielders hitting the cut-off man and executing relays. In short, the team should be prepared to play fundamentally sound baseball. The overall game plan for a winning team over the long haul of the season should fit the caliber players you have on the team.

Managers should save the game in the 8th inning and worry about the 9th inning when it comes.

The manager should at times argue with the umpires even if he is wrong just to lay the ground work to get future calls.

Manager must sent runners to avoid the double play

If a hitter continues to miss his pitch, he may have a timing problem. If he continues to play it will be at the team's expense. The remedy is more time in the batting cage, the bench or being sent down to the minor's.

There is no rationale for intentionally walking a light hitting hitter to get to the opposing teams best hitter.

Most managers won't give steal sign to runner on second base. The runner is on his own.

Sometimes the decision to execute a squeeze play depends on what type of the hitter the manager was.

You don't play for a tie on the road.

Instruct your hitters to take the 3-0 pitch

Game seven of the world-series, every pitcher is a reliever.

What could determine if you have a batter bunting in the first or early innings is whether you have a dominant pitcher who can shut down the opposition.

When the third baseman is guarding the third base line with a runner on first, the manager is saying you will need two hits to score a run.

Sometimes when you try to get into the umpires head, you get into the opposing managers head.

When you put a shift on, the pitcher should pitch to the shift.

A four man rotation puts too much strain of the arms of the four pitchers. Now each pitcher only has three days to rest and recover.

On the road, managers may want to bring in their closer in the 8th inning with the score tied.

Late in the game with a two run lead, keep infield back and give up the run.

The manager should have a game plan based upon the opposition. At a minimum, the game plan should entail the following:

- How to get into the oppositions weak bullpen if they have a strong starting rotation
- Does the opposition starting pitcher have command of the strike zone? – If not, instruct your players to be patient
- Try to get opposition pitchers into high pitch count.
- If game is out of hand, do you have utility players ready to play?
- Who's injured on the opposition team
- Can you run on their catcher
- Lining up your defense properly according to the hitter and the situations.
- Does the starting pitcher have a high leg kick?
- Can your runners take a sizable lead off of first base?
- Does the opposition team have outfielders with strong and accurate arm's?.
- Do you have base runners who can take advantage of weak throwing arms in the opposition's outfield?

- Does the opposition have speed on the base paths? If so, does your catcher and outfielders have strong arms to match that speed?
- Are you playing in a spacious ball park? If so, do you have a centerfielder with good speed? If so, have your pitcher pitch to that strength.

In a crucial game, if you get an early lead you keep the pressure on by bunting to advance the runners and by executing the hit and run.

Late in a game and season, managers should match up with every batter (i.e. LHP vs LHH – RHP vs RHH))

A manager may leave in a RHP against a LHH if the pitcher has a good splitter. The splitter moves down and away against a LHH.

If the manager has a good closer for the 9th inning and a good set up man (7-8 innings), if he has a lead, he can shorten the game to 6 innings.

If the starters are not completing games or pitching late into the game, this could put a strain on the bullpen.

If a pitcher has a large lead and is pitching to the score board, if the opposing team scores a few runs, the pitcher should then switch back to a small lead mentality.

If a team has a good hitting pitcher, the manager may want to bat him 8th in the order so that the 9th place hitter can turn the line-up around as the leadoff hitter. (National League)

The manager needs to ascertain that all of his front line and utility players are bunt savvy. You don't want to be in a crucial playoff situation needing to advance the runner with a batter who is a weak bunter.

The manager and hitting coach should be on the same page. The hitting and pitching coach should not make statements to the media which may conflict with the manager's position.

If the team is struggling, they should then convert to small ball with bats and sacrifices.

If a manager is considering using a pitcher on three day's rest, he must further consider if the pitcher has a good fastball, curve and change-up. If so, he may be effective with three day's rest.

If the pitcher is up with 2 outs and a runner on, don't send the runner. If he is thrown out, the pitcher leads off the next inning.

Conditioning is important as pitchers must be in shape to get to the 7th or 8th inning especially with a high pitch count.

There seem to be more players going down with injuries than ever before. Some experts feel that today's player's work out too much. In the last several years there has been a rash of injuries such as arm and shoulder related injuries (forearm and triceps strains). In addition, other injuries include strained obliques, quads, hamstring pulls and back spasms. Those same experts feel maybe it's time to do away with the weight rooms and limit the time spent in the batting cage. The baseball season is long and players need to rest their bodies for two or three months after the season. However, today's players have their own personal fitness coach and work out all winter. In addition, some player's go to the stadium early to take hundreds of extra swings in the batting cage. Player's with muscles that are strung too tight are more susceptible to injuries. Baseball is a game of fluidity, timing and coordination not muscle mass.

Late in the game, with runner on first and pitcher due up, the manager should send the runner. If steal is successful, then the manager can pitch hit for the pitcher.

The manager can send the pitching coach to the mound to buy time for the reliever to warm up.

Managers should ascertain that they are never without a backup catcher and perhaps a back up to the back up.

With 2 outs and a runner on first and a pitch hitter hitting for the pitcher, an attempted steal with the runner being thrown out would be a wasted use of the pitch hitter.

During extra inning games, managers should instruct batter's to stop swinging at first pitches. Take a few pitches. You are most likely deep into your bullpen. You don't need a quick 1-2-3 inning further exposing your bullpen.

With 2 outs, walking the 8th place hitter (National League) in front of the pitcher is not a problem. Worst case the opposing manager pinch hits for the pitcher (most likely move anyway) and you get into the bullpen.

Lenzy Kelley Jr.

It's not a good idea to steal in the first inning when the pitcher has not found the strike zone. If the runner is thrown out, you have helped the pitcher who is having control problems.

If your pitcher has a high pitch count and is coming up to bat (National League), the hitter in front of him should take a few pitches and try to go deep into the count.

Do not bring in your number #1 closer in a tie game on the road, unless it's the play-off and you're down 2 games to none.

If a team has a weak bullpen, you won't get into it if your hitters are swinging at the first pitch

If one of your hitter's is fouling off good pitches, checking his swing, reaching, off balance and late, then he is obviously having some problems and should be deferred to the batting coach for a remedy.

If the starting rotation is not doing the job, then reduce the number of innings they pitch by shoring up the bullpen and make it a 5 inning game. Have strong middle relievers for innings 6-8 and a closer for 8-9.

For a 0-2 count, take the bunt off.

Have first and third basemen guard the line late in the game.

If the opposing team has been off a few days, have your pitcher go after them with fast balls.

When you make whole sale changes, make sure the game is in hand.

If you have a large lead and are in cruise control, your team may lose their edge.

During the regular season, the pitch count is important. Not so important in the post season. However, a high pitch count gives the opposing team more chances to observe the pitcher.

With two outs and lead-off man at bat, send the runner's. If thrown out, you still start the next inning with your lead off guy coming up.

The team that has to fight to the last game is battle tested and ready for the play off's.

If you are making a pitching change and plan to bring in your closer, if you also plan to IW the next batter then let the pitcher being replaced walk the batter. Do not use your closer for the IW of the first batter he is to face.

With your big bat up, the runner in first should not attempt to steal. If he steals 2nd then the opposing manager may IW your best hitter.

Some managers would prefer not to have runners moving with their best hitter up.

Managers must have a game plan and personnel ready to play when his best player goes down with an injury.

If you play for no doubles then there will be a gap between 3rd base and SS and 1st and 2nd base.

When constructing the line-up, the manager should consider the follows:

- Lead-off hitter, can handle the bat, has a good eye, has speed, can bunt, able to beat out infield hits, runs the base paths well, can steal and has a good on base percentage.
- Number 2 hitter-all of the above as cited for the lead-off hitter, can move runner's over with speed to stay out of the DP.
- Number 3 hitter-hits for average and is able to drive runs in.
- Number 4 clean-up hitter-a power hitter, able to drive in runs with a low strike out ratio.
- Number 5 hitter-also a power hitter able to keep opposing pitcher from pitching around the #4 hitter.
- Number 6 hitter-same as number 1
- Number 7 hitter-same as number 2
- Number 8 hitter- same as number 3 but also a good runner with pitcher due up next
- Number 9, Pitcher (NL), DH (AL) The DH does not have to be the number 9 hitter and can be placed anywhere in the line-up. The DH could be a veteran player who can no longer field, has a weak throwing arm, lacks speed but can still hit. Could also be your clean-up hitter.
- Managers should provide extra BP for pitchers so at the very least they would be able to bunt and move runners over. Pitchers should not be an automatic out.

When constructing the line-up consider that there are some purest who do not like lefty-lefty and would prefer a righty-lefty-righty combination through-out the line-up. This is only possible based upon your personnel.

As left handed power hitters are in short supply, be careful not to load up on too many RH power hitters. Doing so may set you up to be shut down from the 6th inning on as the opposition brings in the shut down power RH pitcher/closer with the 95 mph fast ball.

A line-up laden with free swinging power and pull hitters is an un-balanced line-up. You need place setters who get on base and at least two batters who can drive runners in.

Hitters who drive a lot of runs in most likely have more opportunities. As such you will need at least two on base machines batting in front of your RBI guy.

If a team is aggressive on the base paths without running into outs, they become a better team and score more runs.

Always keep the DP in order. Don't let the trailing run get in scoring position.

The manager needs to determine if he wants his 2-3-4 place hitter's sacrificing runners over (as opposed to 7-8-9 place hitter's). The decision should be based upon the inning (early or late in game) and score.

With a 3-0 pitch, late in the game, behind 1 run with your best hitter up, the manager must give the hitter the green light if the pitch is good.

Bad base running will run you out of a rally.

Managers should grow into good in-game managers that understand the flow of the game and don't lose games because of their in-game moves.

Managers should pick their spots to get tossed from the game. If they have to be thrown out by the umpire to get the team fired up, then there could be other more deeply rooted problems.

Managers must find a way to win close games.

Your team must beat the bad clubs. You must win the series 3-0 or at the very least 2-1.

If it's raining, you play the 4th inning like it's the 7th inning. (Small ball)

A speed person should be batting in the 8th position in front of the pitcher (National League) as the pitcher most likely will be bunting.

If you don't have a speed runner on 1st, don't hold him on. Have your 1st BM play behind the runner. Holding him on creates a hold between 1st and 2nd.

If the number 3 hitter and clean-up hitter continue to leave runners on base and not drive them in, then perhaps it's time for the batting coach and hitter to go to the video tape to find out why and make corrections.

In choosing the starting catcher, managers may want to overlook a weak bat if the catcher is durable, can play through pain and injuries and has a strong throwing arm.

Have your pitch hitter simplify his approach and not try to do something dramatic.

If an aging veteran player is having a hard time catching up with the fastball, it may be time for him to choke up on the bat and cut down on his swing. This is a difficult decision to make especially when it concerns a popular veteran player. However if you have an aging RHH who can longer catch up with the FB from a power RHP, you may need to pitch hit for him in later innings or platoon him and just play him against lefties.

When trading for a power hitter you must consider the ball park he just left and the one he's coming to. His home runs in the old park may be deep fly outs in the new park.

Managers must not be reluctant to call out veteran or star players who do not hustle or who have attitudes issues. Lack of hustle and bad attitudes can infect the entire club house.

Managers should impress upon their team that they can't pick and choose when to bring their "A" game. They must bring their "A" game every night.

When facing opposing dominate "lights out" pitchers, your team has to be patient, work the count, and extend at-bats to build up the pitch count in an effort to get him out of the game. If you wait for elite pitchers to make a mistake, you'll be looking at a complete game shut-out. However, when the count is even or if the hitter is ahead then they must become aggressive in order to do any damage. If the opposing team has a weak bullpen, then you need to get into the bullpen.

Managers, bench coaches and scouts should identify the opposing hitters who are good east and west hitters. To those hitter's, pitch then north and south by changing the eye level as opposed to pitching him east and west.

Lenzy Kelley Jr.

Managers and pitching coach should remind their pitching staff not to get cute and attempt pitches that are not in their skill-set.

If your pitchers are working around a particular hitter in the line-up, they need to make sure that they minimize the impact of the other hitters that follow the hitter you're pitching around.

If the opposing team is weak defensively then your team has to put the ball in play and force them to defend and make plays.

On the road, do not bunt to tie unless you have an outstanding bullpen.

With your best batter up, don't take the bat out of his hand with an attempted steal.

In making a pitching change, manager's can stall by waiting for the umpire to come to the mound.

Managers must prepare their team for the long grueling baseball season. The season is a marathon not a sprint. Do not play your "A" team every day. Have secondary utility type players that you can plug in without degrading overall team performance. Have a good physical trainer that will have your players in excellent physical condition. Remind players with muscular lower bodies to properly warm up to avoid groin injuries.

Older veteran players may become fatigue during the Aug-Sept time frame. See above comment re: able utility players.

During the dog days of summer, managers should ascertain that his players are properly hydrated. Sodas and soft drinks don't count. Players must drink ½ their body weight in water every day.

Remind players to watch their diets by loading up on fruits and veggies. Eat balanced meals with protein from meats. Confine meat intake to bake chicken, turkey, fish and lean pork. For bacon lovers, try Canadian or turkey bacon in-lieu of pork bacon. Also try wheat or multi grain breads instead of white bread.

Stay away from sugary drinks and empty carbohydrates

Substitute white rice and pasta with brown rice and whole wheat or multi-grain pasta.

Marathon runners eat pasta and or pancakes before an event for energy, this is good, but try multi-grain to slow the blood sugar spikes.

The team doctor can also be the team dietician

Have regular weigh-ins to check player's weight. If players are carrying too much weight, this could lead to an injury which could impact the entire team.

Managers should remind his team that there is no off season. It's every player's responsibility to stay in shape during the so called off season. It's also every player's responsibility to report to spring training in shape. Be prepared (manager) to levy heavy fines to players not in compliance. The time lost getting into shape could be better utilized for the film room, batting practice and review of fundamentals. Not to beat a dead horse but if players are not in shape at the start of spring

Lenzy Kelley Jr.

training, they risk injuries as they attempt to get in shape prior to the start of the regular season. Injuries to key players will affect the overall team performance. This could be a problem with veteran players who may feel they've earned the right not to work out at the end of the season. Rookies won't possibly be that stupid.

Managers should recognize when their pitchers have tired. Do not wait until they are in a jam before pulling them out. Some pitchers are lights out for 5-6 innings then hit a wall. Managers must recognize the wall.

An injury to a key player will affect the entire team. Don't have your ace pitchers shagging balls in the outfield. Remind your players to avoid other sports such as basket ball and touch or flag football. Also tell your players to spend some of their money and hire repair people to do repair work around the house. Avoid ladder's, roof top repairs, anything with glass, saw's and drills. Lastly, no drinking/drugging while driving or boating. Finally, float the threat of an un-announced urine test to keep your guys on their toes.

For players who come to camp over weight, sit them down and have a civil conversation about how he is to obtain his required weight. Yelling, screaming or threatening won't work. It will only make the matter worst. Also you cannot fine a person into losing weight. Get the team Doctor involved and lay out a reasonable diet plan and exercise routine.

Managers should instruct pitchers to go after hitters recovering from a hip injury or hip surgery. The front hip is extremely important to a hitter (RHH) as it takes all the torque, turning and twisting force. If the left hip is not turning and rotating with force you can't hit with power. A power hitter will have to adjust his swing. A power hitter recovering from hip surgery may not be a power hitter again but he can still be productive if he makes adjustment and hits with his hands. (Bottom line, show no mercy)

Managers should impress upon their players to go after the good elite pitchers early before they get into their groove. To beat them you got to get them early.

Managers should direct their players to stop swinging for the fence during an extra inning game. Just try to put together a few hits to score the go ahead and possible winning run.

Managers normally won't call for a bunt with a high FB pitcher. However, depending on the score they might.

When facing a rookie catcher and a young pitcher, the manager should have his runners stealing to apply pressure.

Managers should caution their players to taper their celebrations to avoid un-necessary injuries. Levy stiff fines to violators

Managers should also caution their players to control their anger to avoid un-necessary injuries (slamming helmets, bats and punching walls and lockers). Levy stiff fines to violators

Managers should also warn players to control their anger and avoid slamming walls, wall lockers, water coolers and breaking bats. They could injure not only themselves but other players. Self inflicted injuries can impact the entire team and if key players are on the

IR list too long, it could impact the team's chances for making the play-offs. Even injuries to utility players can impact the team as these players are utilized to give rest to the every day players.

Managers must stop the epidemic of player's not running to first base. Once the ball is put in play, you don't know what will happen. A potential out could turn into an error. If the batter doesn't run to first, the opposing team's fielder's have an opportunity to recover from the error and throw the runner out. Managers should impose stiff fines for violators. Pete Rose once said that hustle makes things happen. Hustle puts pressure on the defense to make plays, extends innings, produces extra runs and wins close ball games, which ultimately could be the difference between making the play-offs and advancing to the championship game.

Some players have a habit of laughing or smiling when they strike out. There is nothing to laugh or smile about.

Also, some players joke in the dug-out while their team is losing. This is a no-no.

Some players are overly friendly and joke with players from the opposing team while their team is losing. This is an old school no-no.

Some teams have players who are a little eccentric or corky. This is ok are long as it's not contagious and doesn't affect the team performance.

Managers, scouts and others within the organization should make it their business to take good looks at all prospects within their organization. Do not let a player in the minors go un-noticed who then turns up in another organization as a star. Do not be put in a position of having to explain that you had no idea the player had talent.

Managers must rest their older veteran players.

Managers should recognize when veteran players can no longer hit, pitch, field or throw. This could be a problem if the players are approaching records (i.e. homeruns, strikeouts, ECT.)

Managers and hitting coach may want to suggest to players who can no longer catch up with the fast ball to choke up on the bat and take a shorter swing.

If your team is not scoring runs, you need to have your best defense on the field to keep you in the game.

If the runner on first is a threat to steal, managers should show pitch out the earlier in the count the better.

Before managers consider having the batter sacrifice, he needs to consider the talent of his players as a lot of players cannot bunt properly.

Managers may want to give their veteran pitchers a little more leeway when considering if they should be taken out of a game. This will be ok until the pitcher proves that he can't be trusted to be honest. Rookie pitchers get no consideration.

Mangers should ascertain that pitchers take their time during spring training in building up arm strength. They should start throwing at 78 mph and slowly build up to 80, 88, 90....

Lenzy Kelley Jr.

Manager's should have his team practice situational base running to avoid his team running themselves out of an inning, a rally or into a lost.

Managers should ascertain all players know their designated place or position for backing up a play.

Bases loaded with one out, bring the infield and outfield in. The pitcher must induce a ground ball double play or a strike out. To induce the DP throw up and in or low and away. If you get the second out with a strike out, you can now move the infield and outfield back to their normal depth.

With runners on 2nd and 3rd with two outs, with the pitcher nibbling the outside corner, if the hitter is not swinging and the count goes to 3-0, you should then intentionally walk the batter. The hitter is looking fastball and you don't want to groove one.

With one out, a runner on 1st base and the pitcher due up next, it makes no sense to lay down a bunt. Unless you plan to pitch hit for the pitcher, have the hitter swing away.

Managers need to think ahead to determine if the game may likely go into extra inning. If it does, he may want to keep his best hitters in the game as opposed to late inning substitutes. Most late inning substitutes are done for defensive reasons. As such, managers will have to weight benefits of leaving in his sluggers if they pose a defensive liability.

Managers should remind their player's that when running the base paths and rounding a base, be sure to step on the base. Take the guess work away from the umpire in the event of a protest which could go against you and cost your team a win.

Tell your players not to argue with the umpires. That's your job. Some players become too demonstrative while getting in the face of umpires. If you touch the umpire, you get kicked out of the game. A player's removal could affect the game's outcome. If you play nice with the umpires, that may buy you a favorable call during the game or in the future.

Managers should consider having two hitting coaches. One for RHHs and one for LHHs.

Managers and coaches should observe the stadium stands and seats to determine if there is anything that could distract your players when at bat. If so, bring it to the attention of the umpires and the umpires will notify security.

If managers ask the umpire to check the opposing pitcher for a foreign substance, they need to make sure that their pitchers are clean.

Managers should monitor closely the racial climate within the locker room. Tune into and monitor any petty jealousy by white and Afro-America players towards Hispanic players who may be viewed as job takers. Let it be known that the players who play are the players who perform. Race will not dictate the starting line-up. Do not allow cliques to form. Do not allow whites, blacks and Latino's to form their own little groups. When assigning lockers, mix and place whites, blacks and Latinos side by side. Implement a music policy which requires players to wear head phones when listening to their music as opposed to having 25 or more players blasting out loud music within the locker room. Also, you can't have 25 guys blasting rap, Latino and country music at the same time. One person's music may be offensive and annoying to others players. Also keep a close watch on card games before and after the ball game. Have a policy regarding time limits and gambling.

Counsel your married players about having girl friends on the road. This is a time bomb waiting to explode and will disrupt the team. As manager, you may personally know the players wife and children. In addition, you may personally know the players girl friend. When the relationship is exposed, you may come off as an enabler. As such other wives on the team may not trust you. This will not be a healthy situation team wise because the player's families are an extension of the team. If there is turmoil within the families, it will eventually spill over into the locker room, thus impacting team performance.

Do not allow players off the field commercial activities to consume them to the point where it affects their on the field performance. Watch this closely. This also includes managers and coaches who must set an example.

Do not allow rookie players (especially those who have just signed a large contract) to roam the city alone (Darryl Strawberry and Dwight Gooden). Assign a veteran player as a chaperon.

If you have players who are constantly late, have a coach or veteran player call them in the morning to ascertain that they are up and in-route to the ball park.

Encourage players to further their education during the off season to have a profession to fall back on when their playing days are over. There's no guarantee that they will have a 15-20 year career. Injuries could cut short their base ball career.

Have mandatory financial counseling for players. The importance of saving and smartly investing money cannot be emphasized enough. Millionaire athletes need to understand that the money they make in five years must last them for the next 50 years. The alternative could be baseball card autographs and signing events where former players will charge anywhere from $25.00 to $100.00 for an autograph. They would probably do it for free if they didn't need the money

Latino players like to engage in what some may call excessive celebration. That's fine as long as they can take it when the other side is celebrating. Also some degree of showmanship is fine as long as it doesn't involve bad decisions.

Managers must impress upon their players to play the game all the way through. The eliminating out is always the hardest. The Mets were one out away from defeat in the 1986 World Series. The Washington Nationals were one strike away from defeating the Cardinals in the NL Division series. No celebrating, popping corks, high fiving or dancing. Keep noses to the grind until the final out. The alternative is the Red Socks of 1986, the Texas Rangers of 2011 and the Washing Nations of 2012.

Managers should instruct their 3rd base coaches not to show any mercy towards the opposing team by not waving a runner around to score during a blow out. The opposing team could rally in the bottom of the 9th inning and defeat you by one run. Play all the way through. Make the opposing team get you out and your team should score whenever possible.

Managers should observe the body language, spoken language and actions of his players when things are going badly. He needs to determine who he can depend on to be discipline and poised when the going gets rough.

If there is bad blood between your team and the opposing team as a result of an on field bench clearing brawl, managers should ascertain that it does not carry over into the parking lot after the game (extra security to keep teams separated).

If your ace pitcher (or any other pitcher) is on the mound and hits the batter, if the batter charges the mound, instruct your pitcher (before hand) to back up and give ground while the 1st basemen or 3rd basemen rush over to intercept the hitter. You don't want your pitcher hurt in a brawl and out for 6-8 weeks with a broken collar bone or any other injuries.

Some managers are encouraging or insisting that their hitters show more patience, discipline and selectivity at the plate. Player's tend to shun this philosophy late in the season as they chase hits and stats. But it appears that someone conducted a study and have determined that if a team see's 150 pitches a game, they have a good chance of winning. Of course the opposing pitcher will have to cooperate. As such, hitters must sort through the pitches they get to find a good one to hit. If the pitcher catches on and starts grooving down the middle of the plate then you'll have to get aggressive. If you get a good pitch early in the count managers should have their hitters pulling the trigger and not going to the plate looking for a walk.

Managers should caution their pitchers to not pitch to the score board. Pitching to the score board could produce a rally for the opposing team. Don't get out of your game by throwing fast balls every pitch.

Managers should instruct their hitters not to pose at the plate, thereby turning a triple into a double.

Managers should understand when they try to hide a glove (defensive liability), hits, and plays to that glove will be found.

When putting a team together managers need to select plug and play players who can perform without degrading team performance when the starters go down with injuries.

Managers should take players out of the equation when deciding to rest or take a player out of the game. Players will always say they are ok.

When nursing a lead, managers must recognize when to pull his starters and put in his relievers and/or closers. If you pull him too early or too late and don't win the game you will get criticized in either case. Even if you do win the game you may have personal issues with your starter you pulled who didn't want to come out.

If you don't criticize your star players for not hustling on the base paths, you could have problems with your

Lenzy Kelley Jr.

others player's at some point during the season. These problems could poison the locker room

However, for legitimate mistakes don't throw your players under the bus. If you criticize your players, make sure they are sitting in front of you in your office with the door closed, that way there's no misunderstanding or headlines.

Part of your job is to protect your players. With so many young and inexperienced players, a manager should boost confidence not shatter it.

A triple should not become a double and a double should not become a single because a hitter did not hustle out of the box.

Inside the park home-runs are tricky because not all hitters will have the gas once they reach 3rd base to attempt to score at home. But if a hit has triple written on it, that's what you want, not your hitter sitting at 2nd base because he was admiring his hit

After a 10-15 pitch at bat resulting in a walk or a hit, this is a good opportunity for the manager or pitching coach to pay a visit to the mound to give the pitcher time to regroup and compose himself.

The manager and pitching coach should be aware of the pitchers who have trouble adjusting from the bull pen mound to the regular game pitching mound. Not exactly certain as to what the remedy is if any.

Managers should remind their hitters not to argue balls and strikes with the umpire. Normally if something is said to the umpire he will issue a warning to stop.

After the first warning, further comments will lead to an ejection. Since most managers will protect their players, in most cases this will also lead to the manager being ejected.

This is a grey area and may depend on what side of the bed the umpire got up on, but when the manager goes to the mound and signals with his left arm for the LHP, then realizes he made a mistake and then signals with his right arm for the RHP, the umpire may not allow him to change. This has something to do with causing the opposing manager to make a change based upon your initial signal.

Another grey area, when the manager pays a visit to the mound, then steps off the mound and comes back, he may be charged with a 2nd visit causing the pitcher to be removed.

Late in the game with the game on the line and the opposing teams hitter is last year's Triple Crown winner, if 1st base is open, put him on even if you have your best closer on the mound.

Team defense should improve to the extent of cutting in half team error total from the previous season.

Team strike outs must also be reduced. The manager should stress that hitters put the ball in play.

Managers should emphasis to players not to conceal injuries. Players are at times reluctant to report injuries for fear of losing their place in the line-up. Players have to look beyond the individual desire to stay in the line-up and consider the long range impact and what's best for the team.

With the influx of Asians players, managers should instruct the team and other coaching staff members to can the Asians jokes as the new players may not have a sense of humor.

As teams in general start to resemble the United Nations, there should be a "zero policy" for all ethnic jokes. You do not want your team torn apart or divided as a result of a verbal joke or misunderstanding.

Managers should ask themselves are we making good decisions. Are we executing when we need to to? Are we doing the things we need to do in order to advance?

So much of the modern managers job is knowing how to choose your battles and letting go objections to behavior that excite younger players and fans.

Mangers must thrive to get their players to cut down on mental and physical errors. Making the same mistakes over and over cannot be tolerated.

Managers can no longer prod players through the media. Players today are more sensitive to public criticism.

Managers should not make excuses for player's failures. By doing so, you give players something else to blame other than themselves.

Managers should also understand that with some players you will have to kick them in the butt.

You will want a good relationship and the respect of your players. However, when times get tough, some of them won't like you.

Managers must understand that their players may not be the biggest or the strongest. However for baseball those attributes are not a requirement. What must be emphasized is the execution of the basics to a tee.

If rebuilding is necessary do you rebuild of re-load? Management and owners need to determine if they are willing to endure a 5 year rebuilding plan. Also will the fans tolerate it? Rebuilding can be lengthy as its entails drafting, developing young players from the draft and keeping players healthy. In either case, if you have players with bloated contracts, injury history, declining performance and no trade clauses, you are stuck with them as they will be next to impossible to move. This in itself makes re-loading or re-building difficult.

Do not abuse your relievers from June to Sept. When you ask for more in October they will need to have more in reserve.

Managers cannot manage in October the way they manage in June. In a play-off game and you are facing elimination you can't just bring in a pitcher because he's your 7th inning guy. If you have an elite starter ready to go you have to use him as there is no tomorrow. Having set up guys during the regular season is ok. However, come October, it's all about getting outs not what inning it is. Bottom line don't be afraid to use a starting pitcher.

When using a starting pitcher in relief bring him in to start an inning not with the inning underway with men on base. With an inning underway and men on, he'll have to start by pitching from an unfamiliar stretch.

During the play-off's it's all about who's hot. During the regular season showing trust in your people is fine. However during the play-off's you have to go with who's hot.

Think out the box. What is the opposing manger hoping you will do? Put yourself in the other dugout. What does the other manager dread the most? Do it.

Lastly, managers have to deal with the media and the public. In doing so, they must show poise, class, dignity, respect, knowledge of subject matter and a smile (not phony but genuine). Managers won't always like answering certain questions. Reporters will squeeze you for inside sensitive inside information about your club in general, player's, pitching rotation and injury availability specifically. But you cannot go off into an expletive filled rant towards the media. Hearing the same questions over and over again may irritate you but you need to understand the role of the media in their day-to-day job.

In summation, when putting a team together in spring training the team that goes north should have a dependable pitching staff with a dependable set man and closer who can handle the closer role. Don't wait until the last moment to determine who the 5th starter is, who's in the pen and who the back-up catcher will be. Pitchers should be able to throw strikes with a low walk average. Pitchers must be able to avoid extended stretches of inconsistency. The team should have a dependable long relieve pitcher. The line-up should have consistent hitters who are not streaky. The team should have a good lead-off man with runners who are a threat to steal and outfielders with speed and strong throwing arms. If the right and left fielder lack speed then the center fielder must have speed. Hitters should have a good sense of the strike zone. The team should have reliable and dependable reserve role players. The team should have a solid back-up catcher with some pop. Your best hitter should have some protection batting behind him. If you don't have power hitters, then be prepared to play small ball. Bottom line is that players have to be able to throw, hit and run, hit the cut-off man, show some interest in the game, hustle and avoid taunting opponents and the umpires. Also remember not to over think the game and your decisions. If you call for a pinch-hitter and he strikes out, you're criticized for making a bad decision. If he hits a home run, you're a genius. Lastly, you will need dependable back-up role players in the event one or more of your first stringers goes down with an injury.

If you need to bring players up from the minors, remember, the jump from triple A to the majors can be difficult.

OUTFIELDERS

The center fielder should not dive for a ball unless he is backed up by the right or left fielder.

At the crack of the bat, outfielders should stay neutral or frozen until they get a bead on where the ball is going.

If a runner takes a wide turn at first or third, with a good strong accurate throw, outfielders have an opportunity to thrown the runner out.

Outfielders with strong throwing arms can slow down speedy base runners.

Right fielders should give way to the center fielder.

However, if an outfielder is going to attempt a catch off of his shoe then he is better off diving for the ball. That way he can at least stop the ball. If it gets by him, it's a triple or inside the park home run.

On long fly balls, outfielders should use their non glove hand to feel for the wall. This will help to prevent injuries caused by crashing into the wall and also provides a signal as when to leap for the ball.

Outfielders should approach balls with their body in front of ball, not at angles.

Outfielders should take charge of fly balls from infielders as they have everything in front of them.

With runners on, the outfielder must hit the cut-off man in an effort to keep the double play in order.

If you don't have a strong and/or accurate arm, hit the cut-off man.

If you catch the ball deep, hit the cut-off man

When an outfielder is attempting to catch and throw out a runner at any base, he should get a walking start charging into the catch to get momentum and then push off of his back leg during his throw much like a power pitcher pushes off his back leg. Not stop, catch, start and throw.

If an outfielder is playing shallow, they if the ball is hit to their left or right, they can't charge and throw to the plate.

Throwing a runner out is not all arm strength. It's getting to the ball quickly, getting an angle, and positioning yourself to throw the ball.

Outfielders should take correct route to fly ball. The correct route is over and in as opposed to in and over. If the ball sails away and gets by, it's a triple.

On a throw to the plate, the centerfielders throw must be low enough to hit the cutoff man but high enough to get over the pitcher's mound.

The right fielder with a clear view of a pop up has the right of way over the second baseman.

If outfielders don't get the ball back in quickly enough, runners with speed can turn singles into doubles.

Outfielders should be aware of runners who take a wide turn at first base. It is possible to pick him off at first base with a good throw.

With the outfielders playing deep, you're susceptible to the bloop single.

With runners on and a ball hit deep, outfielders should warn each other that the runner is tagging.

Left fielder's can generally play shallow when a LHH is up.

With a runner on second and a hit to right, the pitcher is backing up home plate. If the outfielder throws to third base, no one is backing up third base. If it's a bad throw, the runner will score. As such, the outfielder must understand there's no back-up at third and his throw must be perfect.

Without hitting the cut-off man, the outfielders throw should bounce in front of the pitcher's mound not behind it to afford a better chance of throwing the runner out at the plate.

The hardest play for an outfielder is the line drive hit directly at him that he can't gage.

Throws to home plate should be on the first base side to avoid hitting the runner from third.

With two outs and runner on second running, the outfielder will not have a play at the plate and should hit the cut-off man to hold the runner at first base.

With a pop ball hit into foul territory, the outfielder with a runner on third may consider letting the ball drop if he can't throw out the runner at home.

Outfielders must quickly decide if they should try and cut a ball off and risk it getting by or playing the bounce off the wall.

Outfielders must quickly get the ball back in to the cut-off man. Don't look to see what's happening.

To rob a hitter of a homerun, get to the wall, find the ball and make your leap.

For balls hit in the air near the foul line, outfielders should play through the play in the event, the umpire flashes the foul sign but the ball is actually fair. Do not give up on the ball just because the umpire called it foul.

If a ball is hit down the line, the outfielder should throw the ball down the line to hit the cut-off man.

Outfielders need to get a clean carom and then hit the cut-off man and not look to 2nd.

If outfielders have weak arms, they then must be able to get the ball cleanly and as quickly as possible to the cut-off man.

In a close game or late in the game, outfielders should not let anything get behind them.

Outfielders must be able to look off the ball momentarily and communicate with each other.

With a runner on 1st base, a left handed outfielder moving away to his right has to turn around to throw. Thus, giving the runner the opportunity to reach 2nd

If the center fielder is tracking a fly ball to the wall in left center, the left fielder should back him up by playing behind him in the event the ball caroms off the wall.

Center fielder should play shallow as more balls will be hit in front not behind him.

A good center fielder with speed can compensate for a left fielder and right fielder without speed.

Outfielder moving back will not get off a good throw to home plate or to any base with the where the runner is advancing.

Outfielders must charge the ball in the event the 3rd base coach waves the runner home then there's a play at the plate.

For pop up's to the outfield, the outfielders should communicate with the infielders to take everything in front of them.

Outfielders should throw low throws to the cut-off man to prevent the ball form sailing overhead.

After catching a ball, outfielders who anticipate crashing into the wall, should cover the glove with their other hand to keep the ball from popping out.

Outfielders tracking fly balls need to take good routes and angles not go side to side.

In a spacious ball park, the outfielders must have good speed to catch up with balls hit deep and in the gaps. If they don't have strong arms, they must understand the important of hitting the cut-off man.

In a small ball park, outfielders can play shallow. Doing so will enable them to reach balls more quickly that are hit down the right field or left line. This will also enable them to possibly hold the hitter to a single or make a play at the plate.

Outfielders should be aware of wind conditions in the ball park as wind conditions can affect the flight of the ball and cause it to be misjudged. At the crack of the bat, if the outfielder takes a step in, then determines the ball was hit harder or has added wind carry, he may not be able to catch up with it.

For a ball hit to the outfield and Kareem's off the wall, the outfielder should circle the ball then square up. If he's playing deep enough, he can then run a straight line directly to the hit ball.

Line drives hit directly at outfielders are hard to pick up and gage.

Outfielders must communicate.

If hitter does not have power, the out-fielders should play shallow to take away bloop singles.

Outfielders who drive at a ball backhanded in a catch attempt run the risk of injuring their thumb in the process when they hit the ground.

Balls hit in the air with a lot of hang time is the responsibility of the outfielders. It's much easier coming in as opposed to infielders going out.

Outfielders can freeze base runners by putting up their glove as if to signal a catch.

With the pitcher up, unless he's a good hitter the outfielders should play shallow to take away the cheap hit.

To avoid injuries, outfielders must recognize that they are near the wall once they hit the warning track.

Outfielders who are slow of speed must make a split second decision as to whether to attempt a shoe string or diving catch. If the ball gets by them, you're now looking at a triple or an inside the park homerun. Before attempting such a catch also consider the speed of the hitter and the runners on base. Also consider the speed of the back-up outfielder.

Outfielders going back for a ball hit deep must get back to the wall and time your jump before you jump. Otherwise you will jump too soon and miss a ball that may have been catchable.

Sometimes if outfielders are trying to throw runners out at 3rd or home, they can prolong an inning as runners can advance. If it is not dead certain that a runner can be thrown out, then just get the back into the cut-off man to keep the base runners from further advancing thus creating an opportunity for a big inning for the opposing team.

Chapter 9

PITCHING

The game has changed with an unprecedented rise in strikeouts. The huge increase in strike outs has also incurred a decrease in home runs and runs scored. As such, it appears that baseball has become a pitching dominated sport. To understand why, one must consider the following: crack down on steroids and amphetamines; lack of power hitters coming out of high school; the biggest and strongest players in HS become pitchers and specialized relieve pitchers. With most teams averaging 12-1300 strike outs a season there is no longer any stigma attached to striking out. It also helps if a pitcher knows how to pitch and is able to throw 3-4 different pitches and field his position. The first inning is the most important inning for the pitcher. He has a fresh mount, he must dig in and find a comfort patch and he will face the line-up that the opposing manager has prepared to attack him. The first out is important and the first inning is important. You don't want to get to the 5th inning before you've settled in as it may be too late. The first inning should be played as if it was the 9th inning.

Pitchers should pitch to their strengths. It's not always possible to pitch to a hitter's weakness. Just because a hitter can't hit a slider doesn't mean that you can't get him out with your FB.

Pitchers who take a lot of time on the mound, stepping off the mound, digging holes and delayed deliveries to the plate, run the risk of their infielders loosing focus.

A closer who doesn't try hard to keep runners close may not want to compromise his delivery.

Pitchers have to find their rhythm. Once you get into a rhythm, things just go and you don't have to force anything or think too much.

To stay out of trouble, stay away from the middle of the plate.

If the pitcher is throwing to middle or center cut of the plate, eventually he will get hit.

Even with a 100 mph FB, a pitcher must have a 2nd go to pitch to instill some doubt in the hitters mind.

With a big lead the closing reliever must finish the game. If the manager has to get up another reliever to warm up, even if he doesn't come in his rest period has been ruined.

When pitching in a park with a short right field porch pitchers must stay on the out-side of the plate low. If you must come in, it should be inside off the plate.

LHP should pound the inside corner (at the hands) for RHHs then throw outside and hope the batter chases the outside pitch.

The hardest pitch to hit is the high hard FB just above the belt.

If the pitcher fails to back up the catcher on a throw home, he could block or interfere with the relay home or block the catchers view.

If a hitter is struggling at the plate, he may take a lot of pitches and find himself in a 0-2 hole. Pitchers should take advantage of these situations and not help the hitter out of his slump. Once you get the batter in 0-2, throw some waste pitches out of the SZ and try to get him to chase them. After all, there's a reason why he's in a slump.

To be effective, a pitcher should have different pitches, zones and speeds.

Starting pitchers must flip the line up 2 or possibly 3 times before the manager goes to the bull-pen.

Do not allow hitters to extend their arms.

The pitcher gets the ball, gets the sign and go. Don't give the batter an opportunity to settle in.

Pitcher's should tighten up their delivery into a compact delivery. No arms and legs flaying.

Pitcher's should finish their pitches to avoid putting a strain on their shoulders. When you finish the pitch, you can almost touch the ground. When you don't, you're standing up-right.

For an inside pitch, if the batter shortens his arms he will drive the ball to center field.

Throw cutter inside on the hands to LHH.

On a 0-2 count, waste next pitch.

Pitchers should not tip their pitches i.e. wide glove change up, narrow glove FB.

Pitchers must be able to throw their secondary pitches for strikes. Otherwise when they fall behind they will be forced to come in with the FB. (Hitters will sit on it)

Pitchers must challenge the number 9 hitter

Set up the hitter by speeding up his bat with a FB then throw slider low or any breaking pitch down in the zone and away.

During an infield pop-up, the pitcher must get out of the way and let the infielders handle it.

A good pick-off move from a RHP requires quick feet to turn, pivot and throw. Throw at the bag to decrease the first baseman tag time.

During the delivery, pitchers should hide the ball as long as possible behind glove and leg kick.

If the pitcher is going to throw a pitch 9 inches off the plate then he might as well walk the batter intentionally.

If a pitcher intentionally walks a batter, he may galvanize the next batter due up.

When a pitcher throws behind a hitter, it's the most dangerous pitch as batters may turn into the pitch.

There's a difference between a brush back pitch, throwing at someone's head and throwing behind a batter.

The threat of being knocked down is not what it used to be as most hitters today watch their homeruns.

After knocking the batter down, the next pitch should be away.

Pitchers should square up after their delivery with their glove up near their face in anticipation of a line drive being hit directly towards their face. There have been a number of injuries resulting from pitchers being hit in the head and face by line drives.

If the pitcher notices that an infielder is out of position he should step off the rubber and motion with his hand for the infielder to move to the position that the situation/defensive alignment calls for.

The change-up will get batters out in front of the pitch.

If you have a good change-up, you can get by with an above average fastball. However, your fastball arm action should have the change-up velocity

If you use the change-up inside and outside, you must have good location if you don't have a good fastball.

A curve ball is most effective when thrown at the same level as the FB. The batter will not recognize it's a curve in time to adjust and will swing over the pitch

You can throw a fastball in the middle of the strike-zone or you can throw one high and away from the batter. It's still a fastball. Location doesn't determine the pitch.

If a hitter is a dead FB hitter who can't handle a curve, then throw him all curves

Pitchers can't throw fast balls on all fast ball counts.

Get ahead with fast balls and then get them out with slow speed curve balls.

Pitchers should change arm angle and velocity to keep the hitter off balance.

An up and in fast ball will keep batters from leaning over the plate and reaching out for a pitch away.

Pound low ball hitters upstairs.

Two seam fast balls moves away from left handed hitters.

Make adjustments with the curve by moving up and down the seams.

Pitchers must back up catchers for plays at the plate.

If the splitter is up in the zone make sure it's away.

The splitter is meant to mimic the fastball until it starts to plunge near the plate

Splitter's look like fastballs at the knees until it loses its velocity and the bottom falls out as it drops into the dirt.

If the splitter flattens out, it becomes hittable.

If hitters start to lay off of splitters down and in, the pitcher can then get away with fast balls down the middle.

The key to the splitter is to get it right over the plate but it can't be a strike. It must end up as a ball.

To make the splitter more effective, the pitcher should bounce one or two pitches in the dirt.

Hitters hit hard splitters on top which produce ground balls.

The split finger fastball must have velocity to be effective or the batter will be able to read the pitch.

To make the split finger fastball more effective, the pitcher should try and get ahead on the count especially if he has a good fastball.

The pitcher must establish the fastball down for hitter's to swing at the splitter. The splitter looks like a fastball then drops.

Throwing the split finger FB on a FB count will confuse the batter.

With a runner on third base during a run down, the pitcher should move towards the third base line to help contain the runner

Two seam FB thrown inside to a LHH not only will lock up the hitter but may also cause the hitter to move his hips back and nick the inside of the plate for a call strike.

Two seam FB from a RHP thrown inside on the hands of a RHH is all but un-hittable.

With a good two seam FB, you don't have to have perfect location. You just need to throw it to an area and let it move. With down action it will move away from LHH and induce more ground balls.

You should use two and four seam fastballs on both sides of the plate.

High FBs at 95 mph that climb the ladder are almost impossible to hit.

Four seam fastballs can be thrown harder

Four seam fastball down and in to LHH and away to RHH

Two seam fastballs have more movement

Two seam FBs tail away.

Two seam FBs induce ground b alls and double plays.

The difference between the 2 and 4 seam FB is about 2-4 mph.

If the hitter has a wrist, hand or thumb injury, the pitcher should throw inside to exploit the lack of quickness.

If the hitter fouls a pitch off of his foot, throw the same pitch as he may not swing as hard.

If a LHP stands on the right first base side of the mound and throws a sweeping side arm pitch to a LH batter, he can't pull the trigger on the pitch as he thinks he's going to get hit as the pitch sails back over the plate at the last second. To the batter, it looks like the pitch is behind him.

Split finger fastballs acts like a screw ball to left hand batters.

Split finger FBs start at the knees and then dips down out of the sz. The batter swings on top of it.

To counter a low ball hitter, pitch lower.

The tighter the grip, the slower the pitch

Change speed on fast ball by griping the ball a little tighter.

Change speed on breaking pitches to keep batter off balance. Then try to sneak fastball by.

Left hand pitchers should challenge left hand hitters.

Strike one is the most important pitch as pitchers must stay ahead of batter.

Hitters who have in the past been hit in the head will buckle when thrown a big breaking ball that comes right at them before it breaks.

A good curve ball will tail back over the corner or the bottom will fall off.

To be effective pitchers must be able to throw the curve ball when behind in the count.

Pitchers need to remember that they can fake to 2nd & 3rd base but not to 1st or home.

Ahead in count, on a 0-2 pitch, the pitcher must avoid the center of the plate and go outside to expand the strike zone. Go after the hitter. Don't waste too many pitches hoping the hitter will help you help. 0-2 & 3-2 the hitter becomes more dangerous.

With location of both sides of the plate, the pitcher can now waste a pitch (Hi and in).

For a 2-0 count, go inside and jam the batter. Do not let hitter extend his arms.

1-2 count is a good count for an off speed pitch as the hitter is looking for a FB.

A batter with an open stance see's the ball better and should be pitched to differently (outside and away not inside).

When you come inside to a LHH you should be belt up. Belt low can be golfed.

Some batters have slider speed bats. The pitcher should ID those hitters and serve them fast balls and change up's.

If the pitcher is up in the strike zone it has to be hard. The batter will get a good look but can't get on top of it.

Pitchers should back hitters up with inside fastballs then get them out by getting them to chase curve balls or breaking pitches away.

A 1-2 FB pitch up and away is a set up pitch for a curveball.

If in a jam, step off the mound and slow the game down while you gather yourself.

When a pitcher gets tired his pitches will be up in the strike zone

During the late innings of a game, pitchers should stay away from the inside pitch which could be pulled.

When the count goes 0-2, the pitcher can then throw two curve balls off the plate.

To avoid going 3-2, the 2-2 pitch must be his best fast ball.

From the stretch, pitchers can't get the break on the slider and curve like they do from the full wind up - No leg kick.

To hold a good base runner a pitcher should vary the amount of time he holds the ball in the stretch.

A pitcher with a slide step and no high leg kick and a quick delivery can best keep a runner from getting a large lead off of first base.

In order to throw off the hitters timing, some pitchers will pause or hesitate at the top of their leg kick. The theory is that most hitters are raising their leg when the pitcher is lowering his. A pause or hesitation could affect the hitters timing.

A pitcher doesn't have to pick a runner off. Just throw over to first base a few times to keep the runner close and from getting a big lead.

A high leg kick and a 75 mph fastball do not give the catcher a chance to throw out the runner trying to steal.

A strike-out pitcher does not have to worry about the runner on 1st base as much as a breaking ball pitcher.

Pitcher's with high leg kicks should quicken their delivery.

A pitcher is having location problems with his change-up or curve. If in the National League he could practice those pitches when the opposing pitcher comes up. The pitcher is not likely to hit out a hanging curve unless he's a good hitting pitcher.

If a pitcher is going to stay outside to a batter, he must throw at least one inside pitch to stand the batter up. That way the batter is not hanging out over the plate.

Dryness makes it difficult for a pitcher to grip the ball (sinkers)

With no outs and a runner on second base, throw all around the strike zone but nothing across the middle.

A pitcher will get in trouble if his pitches have no movement and are in the middle of the plate.

Off speed pitches will cause batters to get out front to quickly and hook the pitch foul

When pitchers get fatigued, they lose command.

The pitcher has to keep the batter off balance by changing speeds and moving the ball in and out, up and down to keep batter guessing and not allowing the batter to dig in.

Do not let batter's get comfortable. Vary your pitches. Pitch inside. Step on and off the mound and quick pitch. Mix breaking and off speed pitches. Make them move their feet. Change the hitter's eye level.

Some pitchers get too much movement with pitches sailing back over the plate.

If a batter has lost his bat speed, do not help him out by throwing slow breaking pitches.

Pitchers pitching in a spacious stadium with an excellent defense should let the batters swing away.

If a batter has warning track power, let them him hit swing away.

If a pitcher goes 0-2 to a free swinger, he should then bounce a curve ball in the dirt hoping the batter will chase it.

When the pitcher is 0-2 he can afford to waste 1-2 pitches by gong up the ladder, high up into the strike zone.

Pitchers should pitch to the aggressiveness of the batter.

A cutter looks like a fastball (cut fast ball). An outside pitch will set up the inside cutter.

A cutter will come at you then cut back over the plate.

A cutter starts off looking like a sinker. The hitter thinks it will break down but it breaks back across the inside corner.

High cutters that don't break can be hit.

A cutter will also start outside the plate about 9 inches and then cut back inside. It's hard to read and hard to hit.

A cutter from a LHP runs in on the hands of a RHH.

Use the cutter in to set up the hitter then punch him out with a cutter away.

If thrown in the right location, the cutters will tie-up a RHH.

The cutter is easier to trust when pitching away. If you make a mistake, it's only a single.

Cutter in and FB away.

Cutter inside must get inside.

Pound in, pound in, pound in and then throw the slider

Depending on the pitcher, some cutters will move in harder and later to a RHH. Other pitchers will throw cutters with more speed or violent down and in action.

Slider from a RHP to a LHH cannot miss. It must be on the corner.

A slider is like a power curve ball

The slider in and change-up outside, keep hitter's off balance.

The slider must have a downward movement. Spins and dips.

A slider is a FB that cuts, spins and dips.

A slider looks like a FB then breaks down & in.

A slider to a RHH must be down and away. To a LHH, it must be down and in.

Keep slider's down and away,

The slider should be thrown a couple mph slower than your FB. It should have a tight rotation and late break which would make it look like a FB for a while.

Slider down and in can be golfed by a LHH

Sliders must go down. If it stays flat, it will be hit out.

A good slider can get out a dead FB hitter.

Aggressive hitters are susceptible to the outside slider.

RHHs are susceptible to the back door slider

Back door sliders from a LHP to a RHH hit's the outside corner and then sinks to the knees.

If the slider is your bread and butter pitch, you must then trust the catcher to block the plate.

A good breaking pitch will have hitters swinging over it.

A pitch right above the belt line makes it difficult for the hitter to get on top of it.

Two seam fastball= sinker

Sinker's low and away to right handed hitters from a left handed pitcher.

A good sinker and curve is especially effective against RHH.

Sinkers drop/sink under the bat and induce ground balls.

Sinkers cannot be up in the strike zone.

Low and away sinkers to RHH and LHH will cause the hitters to beat the ball into the ground.

Don't throw sinker balls to low ball hitters.

Inside sinkers should produce ground balls.

An indication that a sinker ball pitcher is getting tire will be when he starts to miss high in the strike zone. His legs are tire and he is not driving the ball.

Conversely, if a sinker ball pitcher is too strong (too much rest) the pitch will be up and flatten out.

A curve ball back over the center of the plate will be in the hitter's wheel house.

An off speed pitch down and in will speed up the hitters bat.

Pitcher only has to show two seam FB inside once to set up for the outside cutter.

If a pitcher can effectively change speeds and nip corners, he can win without an imposing fastball.

Some pitchers want their catcher set so that the middle of the catcher's chest is in line with the outside corner. Catchers can set up on either side of the plate so that the pitcher can use the catcher's body not his glove as the target. Pitcher's will get more calls from the umpire if the catcher is set up that way and don't have to move the glove to catch a pitch that's an inch or so off the plate.

When a pitcher leads with his elbow and stay on top the pitch will be up and away.

When a sinker ball pitcher gets tire, the sinker ball will rise up in the strike zone. Thus balls are then hit in the air.

For an inside pitch, if a strike, the batter may or not swing at it. If it misses, it's a wasted pitch. An outside pitch allows the batter to extend his arms.

A Left handed pitcher pitching to a left handed batter – Keep low and away. If you get ahead in the count then high and tight.

Some pitchers like to establish their fastballs early. That's fine unless you're facing a team with fastball hitters at the top of their line-up.

After the pitcher establishes his fastball, at 0-2 he should waste an outside curve ball.

During a pop up at home plate, the pitcher should get out of the way and verbally yell (1st, 2nd or catcher) who should catch the ball.

In certain situations (like a blow out) a pitcher should pitch to the score board not the batter.

The pitcher must keep the weakest hitters (7-8-9) off the bases.

The pitcher must bear down to keep the lead-off man off man off the bases.

When a pitcher hits a batter, his offense may then be put on the defensive as they will be expecting to be hit in retaliation and will be bailing out.

Pull the string on hitters with long strides.

A pitchers fastball speed should be constant to maintain the difference in speed between his fastball and change-up.

A 90 plus mph FB and an 85 mph change up is a hard combination to hit.

For power hitters, if you challenge them in on the hands, one inch could be the difference between a walk and a strike.

If you nibble the outside corner the hitter might get inpatient. You also might not get the calls from the umpire and the hitter may not swing.

Pitch down in the zone low and away then explode the fastball.

When the pitcher backs up the catcher, he should be deep behind home plate.

Get ahead with fastball and finish off with breaking pitches.

A down and in pitch can be hit. A down and off the plate pitch will get a batter out.

Down and in to a LHH is not a good pitch unless it's off the plate or drops.

A 0-2 pitch should not be hittable. Keep outside of strike zone.

Pitchers should have a third pitch against the good hitting teams. (I.e. off-speed curve)

If a pitcher throws a curve the catcher should know its coming.

To be effective, the relieve pitcher must get the first batter out.

The long reliever must be cable of keeping his team in the game while his team chips away to get back into the game.

If you have a mid 90s fastball, use it to set up your breaking pitches.

When you're wild, hitters can sit back because they know that you'll have to throw a fastball for a strike. See next comment

A pitcher must be able to throw breaking pitches for strikes.

A pitchers motion should not alert the batter as to what pitch is coming.

In the National League, 2 men on, 2 outs, number 8 hitter up. Walk him to get to the pitcher or a pitch hitter. (Forced the opposing manager to make a move)

A pitcher can be effective with two pitches (i.e. fastball and curve) if he uses the same arm slot

If a pitcher has never faced a team before, he should not show all of his pitches the first time through the line-up.

With 2 outs, bases loaded, and a 3-2 count, the pitcher should pitch from the stretch not the full wind up. This way with the runners going, the runner on first will not score on a single.

LHP to LHH, pitcher should move him off the plate to open up the plate for outside curve ball.

LHP to LHH on a 1-2 pitch must put the batter away on that pitch. If not, the batter will expect and look for a better pitch to hit.

The pitcher must load up on his back leg otherwise he short arms the pitch.

Pitches up in the strike zone will get pitchers in trouble.

If you have a good fastball, challenge the batter. At best, a batter hits 300 (3 hits every 10 at bats). Make him put the ball in play.

A pitchers foot work on the mound should be even and consistent. After delivering the pitch the pitcher should be facing home plate with both feet even with glove up in the event of a come-back. The pitchers delivery should not have him falling towards first base or third base.

Some pitchers throw with such velocity that their momentum has them falling towards the first or third base line. Pitchers should try and square up after the pitch delivery.

Pitcher's who throw across their bodies will have their landing leg cross the stationary leg (off balance). Not a good position to handle come backs or bunts to the opposite side of where the momentum is taking him.

A change-up is most effective with the same arm motion and release point as the Fastball.

The change-up should be followed by the FB to give the batter a different look.

A change-up will make the FB more effective

You want the change up down and in. Throw it hard and let the grip and arm action do the work.

To throw a change-up, you gripe the ball with your middle and ring finger. It may feel like it will be hard to throw with any speed. However, first work on the control and the speed will come later.

If a hitter is looking fastball, the pitcher should pull the string with a change-up. If the batter hits the pitch, it will likely be a weak fly ball.

If a hitter is hot, throw something out of the strike zone. As he is swinging a hot bat, he will be aggressive and go after bad pitches.

A change-up from a LHP to a RHH is less effective as it goes down and in. It goes down and away to a LHH

Stay away from the change-up early in the count as it taxes the arm and increases the pitch count.

Good fastball hitter's have trouble with breaking balls and change-up's

If a pitcher is not a hard thrower then he must hit the corners.

For dead pull hitter's who like to extend their arms, you pitch them tight on the thumbs and low and away.

Late in the game and the pitcher has gone through the whole line up twice, this is a good opportunity to show a pitch you haven't thrown yet.

If the runner on first is not a threat to steal then there is no need for the pitcher to slide step towards home plate. Just do normal delivery.

RHP like to throw two seam fastball to LHH because it tails back over the inside corner.

A fastball will look a little faster after a slow curve ball.

LHP who come across their bodies are effective against LHH. This is because the hitter cannot dig in as seems that the pitchers arm is behind him. Problem is LHP who pitch across the body cannot throw strikes consistently. However, the across the body pitcher makes a curve very effective.

Throw one or two slow curves then change the batters eye level with a high fastball.

The pitcher should pitch to the target presented by the catcher. If the catcher is set up for an outside pitch, don't throw an inside pitch.

Pitchers must make hitters swing at the pitchers pitch, not down the center of the plate. A 0-2 pitch cannot be down the middle. Make hitter chase your pitch.

With two outs and a runner on second base, the pitcher should concentrate on the batter.

Pitchers will develop blisters where the thumb rubs against the seam of the ball. Pitchers have to develop callous.

To get rotation, pitchers need to grip the seam.

The key to a good change-up is arm speed.

If a hitter knows that a pitcher cannot throw a certain pitch for a strike, they won't swing.

When a pitcher throws a breaking ball, it should be a quality pitch, not just to get it over the plate. That's when you hang a breaking pitch that gets pitchers in trouble.

High and tight, low and away. In and out, up and down, fast and slow to get batters out. Nothing thrown across the middle.

Get your breaking ball over when behind in the count.

Do not let down when you pitch to the pitcher (National League). Go after them. Make them put ball in play early in the count.

Pitchers should pitch to the score if you have a big lead. Even if you give up 2-3 homers, you should never go deep in the count. This increases the pitch count and puts a strain on the bullpen as the manager may get someone up.

Breaking balls should be down and in. If pitch doesn't bite enough, batter gets a better look.

A breaking ball on an a fast ball count will have the hitter out in front of the pitch.

To be effective, a LHH must be able to get the breaking ball over to a LHH.

A breaking ball that looks to the hitter to be slightly outside the plate then breaks back in to nip the corner is an effective pitch.

When a hitter has a long swing or stride, the pitcher should pitch inside and close.

If a pitcher stays in on the hands, it will make breaking pitches more effective.

Up and in is tough for a batter to hit.

Be careful going down and in to LHH.

For a LHP facing a LHH, if the pitcher stands on the rubber near the first base side, to the batter it looks like the pitch is coming right at him. In addition, the pitcher has more of the plate to work with especially if the LHH is standing off the plate.

A LHP working on the third base side of the rubber gives a LHH a good look at his pitch

To be effective, the pitcher must be able to change speeds when behind in the count.

Pitchers with a wide stance in the stretch cannot generate power as they push off the mound. The power will be mostly arm strength.

If you're going to pitch inside, come inside high. If you come inside low the batter has a better chance of getting the bat head around on the pitch.

Be careful throwing the 3-1 pitch inside as the batter is looking for something to drive. This is a dangerous pitch. The pitcher must be able to throw a breaking pitch and not groove a pitch over the plate.

3-1 is a hitter's pitch. The pitcher should deliver a change-up or an off speed pitch as the hitter is looking for a fast ball.

Pitchers can't always power their way out of trouble. Sometimes, they must use a curve or change-up.

The change-up is a much better off speed pitch then the curve ball because the curve ball can be recognized and adjusted to. The Change-up is like a fast ball. However, by the time you recognize it, it's too late.

A pitcher cannot throw 4-5 breaking balls in a row.

A pitcher must change speeds and eye level to keep hitters off balance.

If you can get your curve ball over early in the count, you should be able to put the hitter away with a hard slider.

Unless, the runner on third base has great speed and is a threat to steal home, with the bases loaded, the pitcher should pitch from the full wind up not the stretch. In general pitches from the stretch are not as effective as the pitcher exerts less drive in the pitching motion.

Just because a hitter likes a pitch in a certain spot doesn't mean that you can't throw it there. You just have to expand the zone a little. Get the batter to go after the pitch he thinks he likes.

Pitchers should mix it up. Pitch outside, inside and up the ladder.

When a pitcher walks a batter, he may feel the need to re-establish the strike zone. As such, the batter may be looking for a good pitch to hit.

On a pick-off move to first, the delivery should be the same as to home plate.

When you jam a hitter, it's hard for the hitter to get out of the box quickly. As such, you run the risk of hitting the batter. So if you send a purpose pitch inside, consider the consequences of putting a runner on if you hit him.

A knuckle pitcher to be effective must pin point his knuckleball better than his FB.

When you pitch traditionally, everything is about driving with your legs. Not so for knuckle ball pitchers

To cut down on the spin on the ball, knuckle ball pitchers must avoid throwing across their bodies like a typical pitching motion. You must take back on your delivery.

A knuckle ball pitcher does have to pitch around a batter as the knuckle ball will dance around the batter.

The knuckle curve is a curve ball with more rotation.

A good knuckle ball pitcher should pound the strike zone and let the knuckle do the work.

The term knuckle ball is a misnomer. The pitch is actually thrown with the fingers.

Slower pitches from a knuckle ball pitcher are easier to pull.

To cut down on the spin of the ball, knuckleball pitchers must avoid throwing across their bodies like a typical pitching motion. When you pitch traditionally, it's about driving with your legs. However, it's different with the knuckleball.

Pitcher's should recognize how a hitter is swinging. If the hitter is slow or behind the FB then show or stay with the FB. Do not help the hitter out by throwing a slower pitch. If he's out front, then throw a slow curve.

Pitcher's who open up the shoulders too soon, will miss outside of strike zone. You do not want to guide pitch over the plate.

Pitchers should not allow hitters to hang over the plate.

When a hitter crowds the plate, if he pitch goes inside, the pitch cannot miss otherwise it will float out over he plate.

Pitchers should learn to pitch backward and not throw pitches expected for a certain count or situation. This will help keep the hitter off balance and from digging in.

Hitter's who have trouble with curves and change-up's may be conscious of those pitches and be susceptible to taking a first pitch fastball.

Expand the strike zone for hitter's who swing at bad pitches.

Curve balls and breaking pitches put pressure on the arm. Pitchers' should use the fast ball for location and the curve ball/breaking pitch for close out.

A curve ball up will get hit.

A hard thrower mush develop an off speed pitch to go with his fast ball. On a fast ball count, hitter's will start the bat early thinking fast ball.

A good two pitch combo is the fast ball inside and slow curve outside.

Pitches up and in and tight around the letter's are hard to hit.

Pitcher's should change the eye level of the batter by moving his pitches up and down.

Pitcher's cannot double up on pitches. If you show a curve ball then follow with another curve ball, the hitter has adjusted his eye level.

If the pitcher does show the same pitch, it should be from a different arm angle.

When a RHP pitches to a LHH inside, the pitch cannot sail back over the plate.

You cannot pitch down and in to LHH. The pitch should be up and in.

If the hitter has a hitch in his swing, it will take him longer to get his bat head through the strike zone. As such, feed him high fast balls.

Do not rely on fast ball when behind in the count.

For a tap back to the mound, to turn a double play, the pitcher does not have to wait on the second baseman to reach second base. He can lead the second baseman to the bag to start the DP.

An effective change-up should have the same arm speed as the fast ball. Halfway to the plate, the hitter thinks it's a two seam FB. But it run out of stream as it reaches home plate at about ankle high and just off the corner some 6-8 miles slower than the FB

Even with a great fastball, to be successful, a pitcher should have at least two off speed pitches he can throw for strikes.

When a pitcher falls behind in the pitch count, they cannot throw a fastball down the middle. They must continue to pitch at the corners and hope the batter swings at a pitch out of the strike zone.

Low and away pitch should induce a ground ball if not hit through the infield. For a pitch down in the strike zone the batter has to reach for it. Up shoulder level over the plate is hittable. Up and away, a good strike out pitch.

Pounding the ball inside can open up the outside corner and prevent the batter from extending his arms.

Pitcher's who don't pitch a lot don't always have command of their pitches and are susceptible to giving walks.

For the little guy with warning track power, throw ball across middle of the plate. Him hit fly balls to deepest part of the field.

The relieve pitcher with a lead in the 9th inning with the opposition needing base runner's, the hitter's will be taking all the way. Do not fool around with breaking pitches. Throw FB strikes down the middle as the hitters are taking.

Pitcher's should get ahead in the count then throw secondary pitches out of the strike zone.

Pitcher's should throw breaking pitches off the plate to inpatient hitter's.

For a pitch inside off the plate, if the batter hit's it, he will hit it foul.

Come backs to the mound should be knocked down by the pitcher to keep the ball in front of him for a short throw to first.

Fast ball inside on the fist will rob hitter's of their power.

Some pitcher's use a slide step to hold the runner at first. The no kick motion takes less time.

To combat the squeeze play it's important for the pitcher to get a first pitch strike.

You cannot walk the batter trying to squeeze. Let him bunt.

If the fastball velocity is not there, the pitcher must determine which one of his secondary pitches is working that he can throw for strikes.

The pitcher must spin towards second with a runner on second just to cut down the lead by the runner.

The pitcher must work both sides of the plate.

By moving a hitter back, you take him out of his comfort level and zone, which will may allow you to get away a pitch later in the game.

There should be at least a 10 mile difference between the fastball and change-up to get batters out in front of pitch. (i.e. FB 90 and CU 80)

If the umpire tightens the corners, and not give that strike, you must be prepared to start pitching more aggressively inside

If a pitcher has several different pitches in his arsenal, it keeps the hitter guessing what's coming. Sliders, cutters, overhand curve and a FB will contribute towards a pitcher's effectiveness.

Some hitters have ego's will not allow themselves to hit singles to the opposite field all day. They want to hit home runs, extra base hits and drive in runs. So they are waiting for pitchers to hang one that they can hit good. But when you pitch down and away you get your ground ball and pop-up.

Pitchers should also learn to read a hitters body language. Your next pitch could be determined by where you throw the previous pitch and how the hitter reacted. Read body language and try to stay one step ahead of the hitter. What the hitter does dictates what you do. In addition, read scouting reports on hitters. If a hitter has a weakness, exploit it. Let hitters get themselves out.

Pitcher's should stay alert on the mound with runners on base. With a speed runner on third, do not turn your back to home plate while cleaning your cleats. Even with slow runners, stay alert.

Pitchers should show batters their curve ball even if they are not getting it over the plate. But don't hang one.

For pop up's near home plate, pitchers should get out the way and not interfere with the catcher.

Pitchers should avoid getting involved in run down's, Let the infielders handle run down's. Pitcher's will only muck it up.

If you're pitching erratic, you won't get close calls from the umpire.

With a speed runner on 2nd base, pitcher must hold runner close.

With runner on 3rd with a come back to the mount, the pitcher must look the runner back to 3rd

With power hitters, you must change speed, motion, keep the ball away to keep hitter off balance.

The pitchers fielding position should be straight up towards home plate.

Establish the FB early but also establish remainder of pitches as quickly as possible.

After a walk, the next batter up should see a FB as the first pitch (but low and away – not down the pike)

If the pitcher throws a 97 mph FB then throws a splitter, the batter doesn't pick up the spin and his bat head is out in front of the pitch.

With a runner on 3rd base, the pitcher should not throw a sinker or slider in the dirt.

With a 0-2 count, after two breaking balls, a FB off the plate is all but un-hittable.

With a 0-2 count, the pitcher really shouldn't throw a strike

There should be a 10 mph separation between your FB and change-up.

Pitchers with big leg kicks will be run on.

Pitchers should go after the #9 hitter (In AL)

Do not walk the pitcher (NL).

A good change-up should look like a FB for about 50 feet.

The change up is an effective pitch when the count is 3-0 or 2-0 as the hitter is looking FB.

If a pitchers FB, change-up, cutter and sinker are around 80-85 mph, than his curve ball should be slower at around 75-78 mph.

The first pitch to a batter should not be a change-up as there is nothing to change from.

Pitchers cannot go to their mouths while on the mound without permission from the umpire. If they do, it's a balk.

Long, tall lanky LHP'ers who stands on the 1st base side of the mound can intimidate LHH'ers as they are throwing behind the hitter.

Pitchers should change speeds and eye levels.

If the hitter steps away from the plate, the pitcher must pitch through until the umpire calls time out.

Pitch near the strike zone and let hitters chase it.

Get pitches over the plate, not down the middle and change speeds.

If the hitter is leaning over the plate, come inside to straighten him up.

With a runner on base, keep him close, know who he is, does he have speed? Vary your looks, come set then hold. Abbreviate your leg kick.

Non power pitchers must rely on location and change of speed.

Since the change up is a good pitch to run on, the pitcher should throw to first base before throwing the change up.

Pitchers should move their FB around as hitters guess the pitch not see the pitch.

If the pitcher is hit on the arm by a line drive and stays in the game, his arm may stiffen up in the dugout between innings.

On a 3-2 count, the pitcher should not be afraid to go with an off speed pitch as the hitter may be thinking FB.

If you throw a curve on a fastball count and get it over, then follow up with a FB.

With a runner on 1st in a possible steal situation, if the runner is recovering from a broken hand, the pitcher should throw over to 1st several times. The throw will force the runner to dive back to 1st. After diving back to 1st base several times, the runner may decide to stay on the bag or attempt to steal second base.

For deception, the pitcher should throw the change up the same as he throws the FB – Maybe grip a little harder

Cutter cuts down and in.

Back door cutter should be knee high. If up, it could be hit.

FB cutter, if you come inside, you have to miss inside.

If the #8 hitter (National League) is hitting 100-200 average, then pitch to him. If you walk him, you just face the pitcher or a pitch hitter. If you get him out, the pitcher leads off the next inning. The manager could still pitch hit for him.

Don't be afraid to try a pick off on a rainy day. The base may be slippery. If the runner's foot slips off of the bag he could be tagged out.

Depending on your control, you could throw lots of soft stuff early in the count then freeze the hitter with a FB.

Some pitchers prefer starting off with FB then following up with a changeup.

A good pitch combo would be a high FB inside, a high FB at the letters then a curve ball low and away.

Try not to throw same pitch 3 times in a row as the hitter can adjust and catch up with bat head quickness. If you must, then change elevation and angle.

If you throw all FBs, go up the ladder or in and out.

With a base stealing runner in 1st base, the batter will give the runner every opportunity to steal. Thus, he's taking the 1st and possibly the 2nd pitch. The pitcher therefore may have a free pitch or two and could grove one down the middle. The flip side is that the hitter may expect it and swing away.

Pitchers should throw to 1st base to catch runners flat footed off their toes.

With aggressive hitters, expand the strike zone.

Lenzy Kelley Jr.

If a hitter is late with his swing and is fouling off pitches, don't help him by speeding up his bat.

Pitchers holding a runner on 1st base should slide step or shorten leg kick in making delivery to batter. Be careful not to balk.

Pitcher should keep FB down, move it up the ladder, mix it up with off speed pitches, pant the corner and stay away from the middle of the plate.

Pitchers should do their homework to determine hitters who can hit slow stuff but can't catch up with the FB. (Lack bat head quickness)

The pitcher must step off of the rubber before breaking his hands.

If you deliver a pitch and the batter calls time-out, do not throw the same pitch.

Be careful with the high FBs as they tend to flatten out.

If you're going to paint the outside corner, make sure you miss up and away or low and away.

Strike outs will elevate your pitch count. Try to keep your pitch around 15-18 pitches per inning. That should get you into the 7th or 8th inning where the manager can now bring in the set up guy and closer.

Back door curve ball – Looks like a ball on the outside of the plate but at the last second breaks back over the corner for a strike. Pitcher must throw this pitch perfect. If it breaks over the plate, then it's a hanging curve that can be hit

If the umpire expands the SZ with a liberal SZ, take advantage of the liberal strike calls. Pitch to those spots until the umpire adjusts (if at all) to the more conservative or true calls.

Use all pitches so that the batter eyes are constantly moving.

For a bunt or slow tap back to the mound, the pitcher should grab the ball, turn, set, plant his feet and then throw the ball.

Pitchers should take advantage of hitters who are nursing injuries by pounding them with FBs. Do not help them out by throwing slow pitches. Certain injuries can prevent hitters from quickly getting the bat head out front to hit FBs.

If a pitcher consistently throws pitches near the SZ, the umpire may give him the benefit of the doubt for close pitches; then again, he may not. Bottom line, pitchers must gauge how the umpire is calling the strikes and pitch accordingly. Adjust to the umpires SZ and live with it.

Some pitches are not designed to get you out but to set you up for the next pitch.

By working inside constantly, you open up the outside of the plate.

Don't try to jam a hitter with an open stance. They can handle the inside pitch.

Not every pitch goes where it's meant to go. Pitchers must hit their spots (location and movement).

Tailing FB tails back in catching the corner of the plate.

A LHP with a right leg that hangs is hard to steal on. The runner doesn't know if he's going to the plate or throwing to 1st because of the hanging right leg.

Sometimes, a pitcher can shake for effect (shake off a sign) to give the hitter the impression that he will throw something else if he has thrown the same pitch several times in a row.

For a comeback to the pitcher, if the pitcher decides to force the runner at 2nd, the pitcher must ascertain that someone is on 2nd or on their way towards 2nd. The 2nd BM or SS does not have to physically standing for 2nd. The pitcher can throw at the base on a timing play if he sees that someone is approaching the bag.

Throw breaking pitches on FB counts.

Crowd power hitters to prevent them from extending their arms.

Behind in count pitch away.

Ahead in count, pitch inside.

Pitching inside strips a hitter of his power by making him pull his hands inside.

When the hitter has two strikes on him, is the best time to jam the hitter.

A four pitch walk could signal the on-set of problems with the pitcher.

The best way for a pitcher to hold a runner on 1st base close to the bag is by holding the ball.

Jam hitter with a good high inside fastball.

If a hitter is fouling off pitches with line drives, throw a change-up.

If a hitter is known for swinging at bad pitches, then throw him a pitch he can't reach.

Never throw three straight change-ups. The hitter's eye will adjust.

When facing a hitter with a high batting average, do not grove middle of the plate fast balls.

When the pitcher has a genaous strike, he should expect it to be not so genaous late in the game.

When pitcher is is known for throwing down hill, the ball is on top of the hitter very quickly.

When some pitchers are working out of the stretch, there's a tendency to throw down the hill too quickly.

If you are going to purposely hit a batter, do it on the 1st pitch. Don't waste five pitches at 3 and 2 before you hit him.

On a 0-2 count, bounce a curve ball in front of the plate to see if the hitter chases it.

Pitchers must be able to throw off speed pitches on FB counts

If you're not a power pitcher on a 0-2 count try bouncing a change in the dirt to get the batter out.

To be effective a pitcher must work the edges and be unpredictable.

On a throw to first for a possible pick off, make sure the 1st BM is coving the bag. If he's playing off the bag, you've picked him off not the runner. If he doesn't get back to the bag quick enough, the ball is thrown away.

Pitcher's should try to cut down on the number of over thrown pitches. Some pitchers average up to 10 over thrown pitches a game. Over thrown fast balls could cause pitchers to yank the slider too much. Thus depriving the pitch of the nasty break it's known for. By executing best pitch management, pitchers can extend their starts by an extra inning as hitters will be putting the ball into play earlier in the count.

Some pitchers from the east coast have problems pitching in the dry climate found in the south west. Because of the lack of humidity and moisture, they experience problems gripping the ball. The only remedy is just step off the mound, lick your fingers and try again.

Pitching to the score board could translate into a high ERA which may hinder future considerations into Cooperstown.

Having the front shoulder fly open is a common problem with power pitchers who get caught up trying over power hitters. Shoulders should stay square to the plate. Do not wrap your shoulder around by trying to generate more velocity. Stay in line and throw downhill.

If a pitcher turns his back to the plate during his delivery he then has to re-acquire or pick up the target again before making or releasing his pitch.

Groove the ball down the middle of the plate for hitters who don't swing at the first pitch

Relievers must be ready when called upon and must also get the first batter out.

Pitchers who can throw the FB 95-100 mph should know the hitters who will take that pitch mainly because they can't hit it.

However, no matter how good or fast your FB is, if you continue to throw it over the plate, it will get hit.

No matter whom you are when you are constantly falling behind in the count, even if you throw 100 mph, you will get in trouble. It's just tough to pitch from behind.

Even with a good FB and breaking pitch, you need command. No matter how hard you throw you must have command and be able to locate your pitches.

You have to be able to throw off speed pitches for strikes.

You cannot give up hits when you have two strikes on a batter. You have to be able to punch him out.

If you throw a change-up for a ball on a 3-2 count, you may get criticized. If it's a strike, all is well.

You don't always have to throw 97-98 mph. Pitches thrown at 92-93 mph will also get the job done.

Justin Verlander of the Detroit Tigers is all but un-hittable when he's on his "A" game (which is just about always). He gets stronger as the game proceeds. Innings 1-3, his FB is at 90-92 mph. Innings 4-6, his FB is 94-96 mph. From innings 7-9, his FB is 98-100. When you mix in breaking pitches, the hitters don't have a chance and look very bad.

Met pitcher Matt Harvey has a four pitch arsenal (FB, slider, change-up and curve ball) which he shows at 95-96 mph with location. As a tall power pitcher he compares favorably to Verlander because he can drive the ball down at the bottom of the strike zone then change eye levels up with swing and miss heat.

Pedro Martinez threw a curveball, circle-changeup, an occasional slider, and a fastball.

Pitchers when covering 1st base should not step on the bag. Just plant your foot against the side of the bag. If you step on the bag, the runner could step on your foot causing a serious injury.

To avoid a balk call, when in the pitching motion once your hands are moving do not stop or hesitate.

If a ball is nicked up, some pitchers would prefer that the catcher not ask the umpire for a new ball.

Some hard throwers with violent deliveries who light up the radar gun are prone to falling behind on the count and walks. Scale back the velocity and establish command of the strike zone. A below average command of pitches will keep you from pitching in the back end of games.

Throwing a hard FB at 95-98 mph and followed up with a splitter is a tough pitch combination for a hitter to handle.

A hard inside FB on the corner that ties up the batter can induce ground balls especially to hitters who hit to the opposite field.

Stay away from so called waste pitches. Every pitch should have a purpose.

When a pitcher has thrown 4-5 innings of no hit ball, after a hit or a walk he may encounter control problems as he now has to work out of the stretch.

In a suspected bunt situation, the pitcher should momentarily hold the ball to see if the batter commits to the bunt.

Pound the ball in and out with curve and change-up out of the strike zone. Or, soft stuff away and hard stuff in.

If the umpire is consistently calling a pitch a strike, if the pitcher can throw it for a strike then he should use it as his go to pitch.

A 95 mph FB followed by an 85 mph change up is all but un-hittable

The pitcher can shake his head pretending to shake off a sign in an attempt to confuse the hitter

When the pitcher is throwing all of his pitches over the plate for strikes, he's then in the driver's seat with a 3-2 count as the hitter cannot sit on one particular pitch. If he does, he is then at a disadvantage as the pitcher is throwing strikes with all of his pitches.

The four basic pitches, fastball, curveball. Slider and change. Mix these pitches for success.

For a 2-2 count, the pitcher can waste one outside. For a 3-2 count, the pitcher must come in closer to the plate. Thus advantage goes to the hitter.

When older veteran pitchers or pitcher's coming back from an arm injury discover that they can't blow hitters away anymore with the FB, they then must put the work in to develop cut FBs, change-ups and pitch to both sides of the plate to keep hitters off stride.

Some pitchers don't pitch inside because they are afraid to or don't know how. Pitchers are afraid that they may hit the batter or make a mistake inside that's hit out of the park. To be an effective inside pitcher, like anything else you must practice. When you get the proper location, it's all but un-hittable.

Use a hitter's aggressiveness by pitching out of the strike zone.

Bottom line – To be successful a pitcher should get ahead in the count, mix up your breaking ball with your change up and keep them honest with your FB. If you're pitching good don't tinker. Wait until the hitters make an adjustment then tinker.

Chapter 10

PITCH BREAKDOWN BY TOM GLAVINE

Curveball

I throw it occasionally to give a hitter something different to look at. Other pitches are mostly on the same plane, but the curve breaks north to south. Not too concerned about where it is on the plate but it's important that I get a sharp break.

Changeup

I hold it loosely with my middle and ring fingers. With that grip I can throw it as hard as my FB, but it comes out 6-8 mph slower. I like to feel like I'm holding an egg, tight enough that I keep it in my hand but not so hard that I crush it.

SINKING FASTBALL

I grip it with the seams and my natural arm action makes it sink and move away from right-handers. I could never throw it straight as it moves. For this reason I set up on the third base side of the rubber.

SLIDER

I used to try to sweep it but it was easy for hitters to recognize so if I left it over the plate, it was crushed. I later stated throwing it a little harder with a shorter later break so it looks more like my fastball.

A inside slider to a LHH speeds up the bat head.

CUTTER

I throw it off my four seam FB grip and try to get a hard late break in on RHHs. It's a good pitch but it's hard to trust because a mistake could mean an extra base hit.

FOUR SEAM FASTBALL

This is more of a power pitch. I grip it across the seams and I'll throw this once in awhile up and away from RHH and LHH to give them a different look from my sinker

PITCH ARSENAL

- **Fastballs**: Four-seam, Two-seam, Cutter, Splitter, and Forkball
- **Breaking Balls**: Curveball, Slider, Slurve, and Screwball
- **Changeups**: Changeup, Palm ball, Circle Changeup

Chapter 11

TOMMY JOHN SURGERY

TJS has become the go to surgery/procedure for fixing pitchers injured elbows named after former Dodger and Yankee pitcher

Tommy John Surgery is known in medical circles as ulnar collateral ligament (UCL). This is a reconstruction of the elbow that entails a surgical procedure which replaces the ulnar collateral ligament in the elbow with a tendon from elsewhere in the body. This is a common procedure among athletes in professional sports.

Why TJS? Since pitching is an un-natural motion, the arm in most cases looks and becomes contorted. That's because throwing a ball over your head is not a natural motion. During a throwing motion the two main problem issues are the shoulder and elbow. The unusual motion of throwing a ball causes undue stress at both places. Other problems areas are with muscles, ligaments and tendons. Pitching causes tiny tears in these areas from the shoulder to the elbow. When the arm becomes sore, the body is telling a person to rest to enable those tears to heal. Since pitching a baseball is a very unnatural act, an enormous stress level is placed on the elbow. Pitchers throw over hand and side armed at a variety of speeds, angles and twists which the arm was never designed for.

In an effort to prevent injuries, some baseball organizations are trying to identify pitchers who are less likely to get hurt. As such, some experts are saying that tall pitchers are able to use/leverage their height to generate torque so that their arms don't have to work as hard. A smoother delivery is desirable as pitchers with unusual motions put too much stress on their arms. Some scouts also look for pitchers with large back sides as more power in the lower body means less strain on the arm.

Due to major medical surgical advancements, injuries can now be diagnosed and successfully repaired with greater ease. Years ago, many pitchers pitched with pain as they were reluctant to have arm surgery, thinking they might never pitch again. Also year's ago, TJS was not as advanced as it is today. Since 1975, 900 players have h ad TJS with the majority able to continue playing.

As a finale note, it should be noted that there is a school of thought that the increase in these types of arm injuries are caused by pitchers not getting enough work. Today we have pitch counts, innings limitations and specialized roles. This decreases a pitchers work load. Add to that the notion that pitchers today emphasis powers over finesse, these factors only increase the likelihood of arm injuries. It is suggested that pitchers coming off of TJS should take it slow and not try to rush back. In addition, there is a school of thought that pitchers today are babied from the time they play Little League with pitch counts and inning limitations. This continues through high school and college and onto the minor league. As such, they are never allowed to build suffienct arm strength. The great Bob Gibson pitched 17 years and threw more than 200 innings 12 times. In two seasons he threw more than 300 innings. Steve Carlton had a 24 year career with 16 years of 200 or more innings. Sandy Koufax who did blow out his arm pitched for 12 years while throwing for more than 300 innings three times. Today it's a major feat if a pitcher gets close to 200 innings and most young pitchers are routinely shut down in August when they get close to 150 innings.

Chapter 12

LEARNING TO IDENTIFY PITCHES

Four-seam Fastball

85-100 mph

- Fastest, straightest pitch. Little to no movement.
- To grip the four seam fastball, place your index and middle fingertips directly on the perpendicular seam of the baseball. The "horseshoe seam" should face into your ring finger of your throwing hand. I call it the horseshoe seam simply because the seam itself looks like the shape of a horseshoe.
- Next, place your thumb directly beneath the baseball, resting on the smooth leather. Ideally, you should rest your thumb in the center of the horseshoe seam on the bottom part of the baseball.
- Grip this pitch softly, like an egg, in your fingertips. There should be a "gap" or space between the ball and your palm. This is the key to throwing a good, hard four-seam fastball with maximal backspin and velocity: A loose grip minimizes "friction" between your hand

and the baseball. The less friction, of course, the quicker the baseball can leave your hand.

Two-seam Fastball

80-90 mph

- Also known as a Sinker.
- Moves downward, and depending on the release, will sometimes run in on a right handed hitter (RHH).
- A two seam fastball, much like a sinker or cutter (cut fastball), is gripped slightly tighter and deeper in the throwing-hand than the four-seam fastball. This pitch generally is thought of as a "movement pitch" (as opposed to the four-seam fastball, which is primarily thought of as a "straight pitch").
- When throwing a two-seam fastball, your index and middle fingers are placed directly on top of the narrow seams of the baseball
- Next, place your thumb directly on the bottom side of the baseball and on the smooth leather in between the narrow seams
- Again, a two seamer is gripped a little firmer than the four seamer. A firm grip causes friction, which causes the baseball to change direction, usually "backing up" - or running in - to the throwing hand side of the plate. It also slightly reduces the speed of the pitch, which is why most two-seamers register about 1 to 3 mph slower than four-seam fastballs.

Lenzy Kelley Jr.

Cutter

85-95 mph

- Breaks away from a right handed hitter (RHH) as it reaches the plate.

Mix of a <u>slider</u> and a <u>fastball</u>. Faster than a slider but with more movement than a fastball.

- To throw a cutter or cut fastball, you will fastball but get a slight amount of side spin that makes the ball move in or out a few inches.

You do this by moving your fastball grip (usually the 4-seam fastball grip) slightly off-center. Some pitchers bring the thumb slightly up the inside of the ball and the index and middle fingers slightly toward the outside. This gives you a pitch somewhere between <u>a</u> <u>fastball</u> and <u>a slider.</u>

For young pitchers, though, there is a tendency to turn the hand too much toward the slider position, getting a "doorknob" action with the hand that can stress the elbow. The pitcher should leave the thumb directly under the ball and move only the fingers slightly left or right, depending on which way you want to cut the ball. As you release it, think "fastball," and spin the ball hard with your middle and index fingers, just as you would the fastball.

If you're a right-handed pitcher holding the ball slightly off- center to the outside part of the ball, the pitch should move a few inches away from a right-handed hitter ... just enough to get it away from the barrel of the bat. Unless you have a fairly high arm angle (throw "over the top") it will be harder to learn to make the ball move the other way, but try it. Just offset the fingers slightly to the inside, and throw with fastball action.

How To Throw A Cutter ... Like Mariano Rivera

To start, you hold it like <u>a fastball</u>. The cutter grip is a little bit off of center. Throwing it is like a fastball, and right here at about the release point, turn over your wrist.

The idea is, it's got fastball rotation, and at about 59 feet, it cuts into a right-hander for a left-handed pitcher. For a right-handed pitcher it cuts into a lefthander.

- The cut fastball and sinker have the same goal: to make the hitter hit the ball without getting the meat of the bat on it. Both pitches will be more effective if you first establish the fastball. Then, when you throw the sinker or cutter, the hitter will see what looks like the same fastball arm and hand action, and will not be expecting the ball to move.

Splitter

80-90 mph

- Breaks down suddenly before reaching plate.
- A split-finger fastball (sometimes called a splitter or splitty) is an advanced pitch.
- Typically, it's only a good pitch if you've got bigger hands. That's because the pitch itself should be "choked" deep in the hand. This is how splitters get their downward movement. Your index and middle fingers should be placed

on the outside of the horseshoe seam. The grip is firm. When throwing this pitch, throw the palm-side wrist of the throwing-hand directly at the target while keeping your index and middle fingers extended upward. Your wrist should remain stiff.

- Bruce Sutter, one of the best splitter pitchers in the history of the game, says that it is very important to put your thumb on the back seam, not the front seam. This puts the ball out front just a bit more than a fork ball. Then, he says, you just throw a fastball. A very sophisticated and misunderstood point is that the split-fingered fastball should be thrown with back spin just like a two-seam fastball.

- When throwing the splitter, the pitcher will need command of the strike zone in order to get ahead in the count. Being ahead in the count makes the splitter all the more effective as hitters will chase it. Pitchers cannot fall behind and allow hitters to wait on the FB.

Split Finger Fastball

A splitter will literally fall off the table. The secret to a good splitter is having the same motion as your fastball. That's the key to getting swings and misses.

Forkball

75-85 mph

Like a <u>splitter</u>, but with a less dramatic, more gradual downward movement

Curveball (3 types)

70-80 mph

- • Commonly called a 12-6 curveball. The 12-6 refers to the top to bottom movement (picture a clock with hands at 12 and 6).
- The beginner's curveball is a great pitch for younger pitchers. In essence, this pitch does the exact opposite as a fastball. Where as a fastball spins from the bottom to top (which is known as "backspin"), a curveball spins from top to bottom. And instead of leverage coming from behind the top of the baseball (as a four-seam fastball), leverage on a curve comes from the front of the baseball.
- I teach a beginners curveball grip to younger pitchers who are learning a curveball for the first time because I feel that it's the easiest way to correctly learn proper spin. Here's how it works: Grip a baseball leaving the index finger off – like you were pointing at something. (Your index finger will be used to aim the baseball at your target.)
- Next, place your middle finger along the bottom seam of the baseball and place your thumb on the back seam (as shown in the middle picture above). When this pitch is thrown, your thumb should rotate upward, and your middle finger should snap downward while your index finger points in the direction of your target. This, of course, is the reason this pitch is great for beginners: the ball goes where your index finger points. The beginner's curveball helps to align your hand and ball to the target.

Lenzy Kelley Jr.

The straight curveball (or "overhand curveball") is one of the most common breaking ball grips. It's a variation of my beginner's curveball and my knuckle curveball.

A straight curve requires mastery of my beginner's curveball, because many of the same principles that applies to both grips. This doesn't mean that you have to throw a beginners curve (most pitchers actually start right out with this pitching grip). But the beginner's curveball is a good place to start. Then, of course, this pitching grip is the next step. That's because there is essentially no significant difference between a straight curveball and a beginner's curveball, except for the finger placement of your index finger. It should be placed *on* the baseball as opposed to pointed at a target.

The thumb action of the pitch is upward. The thumb rotates up while your middle and index fingers rotate down.

The arm action on this pitch is a little abbreviated at the end. Instead of getting a nice long arc of deceleration and finishing throwing elbow outside of your opposite knee (as with your fastball), you'll want to bring your throwing-hand elbow to the opposite hip. This, of course, shortens your follow through, but allows you to really snap off the pitch.

Another more advanced variation of the curveball is the knuckle curveball (sometimes called a spike curve). This is the curveball grip that I used. Thrown the same way as my beginner's curveball only you'll tuck your finger back into the seam of the ball. Your knuckle will now point to your target instead of your index finger (in the beginners curve).

The difficulty with this pitch isn't from the pitch itself. In fact, most pitchers feel this grip gives them the most rotation – and most movement – of any breaking pitch. However, many pitchers who are learning this pitch for the first time aren't comfortable with the "tucking" part. It's not super comfortable at first to tuck your index finger into the baseball.

This is why I recommend that you spend a few weeks – preferably during the off-season – working on tucking your index finger into the baseball. Do it while you're watching TV or in study hall at school. Once your index finger is comfortable with the grip, you can progress into spinning a baseball to a partner without any trouble.

Note: You've got to maintain short and well-manicured nails – especially on your index finger of the throwing hand – for this pitch to be effective because long fingernails can get in the way of the grip.

One thing you can do is apply a thin coat of <u>nail polish</u> or <u>fingernail strengthener</u>. It's in the women's section where fingernail polish is found, of course. It's shiny (even the matte finish is a bit shiny), but dries clear. And it helps to make fingernails a little tougher. (If you do use it, you really need just apply it to your index finger.)

Slider

80-90 mph

- Breaks down and away from a RHH.

Between a <u>fastball</u> and a <u>curve</u>.

- A slider, behind the four seam and two seam fastball is the fastest pitch in baseball. To promote arm-health young pitches should learn proper throwing and grip techniques. When thrown, the pitch comes off of the thumb-side of your index finger, not your index and middle-fingers. A good slider pitch is gripped on the outer-third of the baseball with the wrist slightly cocked without being stiff. This will enable good wrist snap as the pitch comes off of the thumb side of your index finger thus promoting good spin on the ball. A good grip consists of placing the long seam of the baseball between your index- and middle-fingers with your thumb on the opposite seam underneath the baseball.

Slurve

70-80 mph

- 11-5 movement. Similar to a curve but with more lateral movement

Screwball

65-75 mph

1-7 movement. Opposite of the <u>slurve</u>.

A screwball is thrown just like a fastball until the point at which the pitcher's arm is passing alongside his head.

When learning how to throw a screwball, place your two fingers side by side against the seam, as you do when throwing a curveball ... however, you must place them side by side in the *opposite* direction!

That's because placing them side by side in the opposite direction will force the seams to spin in the opposite direction when you twist your wrist and arm to throw it.

That in effect is how the screwball gets its break.

As the arm moves forward past the ear, you begin to turn your wrist and arm in a counterclockwise manner so that when your arm follows through, it moves away from your body from right to extreme right, instead of crossing your body right to left.

The ball will approach the plate spinning in a manner opposite to that of a curveball. And its break, when thrown by a right-handed pitcher, will be down and away to a left-handed batter.

The screwball is difficult to hit, not because its movement is so unusual by itself but because its movement is so unusual in relation to the pitcher throwing it.

For example, batters are used to right-handers throwing breaking balls that move right to left, and so a "reverse breaking ball" brings an element of surprise and oddity with it.

Throwing a screwball takes time. When you're learning how to throw a screwball for the first time, patience and practice are key!

Changeup (3 Finger)

70-85 mph

Slower than a <u>fastball</u>, but thrown with the same arm motion.

- If you don't have big hands, a three-finger changeup is a good off speed pitch, especially for younger pitchers. The changeup is a finesse pitch. To throw an effective three-finger changeup, center your ring, middle, and index fingers on top of the baseball with your thumb and pinky finger placed on the smooth leather directly underneath the baseball. Hold the baseball deep in the palm of your hand to maximize friction and to "de-centralize" the force of the baseball when the pitch is released. This will help to take speed off of the pitch.

Palmball

65-75 mph

- Ball is gripped tightly in palm.

Just like a changeup, this pitch is slower than a <u>fastball</u>, but thrown with the same arm motion.

- The palm ball (sometimes called a palm ball or four-finger changeup) is one of two or three variations of the changeup. It's an off-speed pitch.
- A palm ball is is gripped by essentially choking the baseball deep in your hand and wrapping all of your fingers around the baseball. It's essentially a four-fingered change-up where the baseball is centered in your hand between your middle and ring fingers.
- The index and ring fingers are placed on either side of the baseball for balance, and the thumb is placed directly below the baseball. At its release point, try to turn the ball over a little to

get more movement. The deeper the grip, the more friction that is created on the ball, which takes off velocity.

- However, as with all off-speed pitches, the arm speed and mechanics of your pitching delivery have to be the same as your fastball.

Circle Changeup

70-80 mph

A changeup with 1-7 moment like the <u>screwball</u>.

- The circle changeup and the four-seam fastball are what got me to professional baseball. They're both great pitches.
- To throw a circle changeups make - quite literally - a circle or an "OK" gesture with your throwing hand (using your thumb and index fingers). You then center the baseball between your three other fingers (as shown in the middle picture above right). The baseball should be tucked comfortably against the circle.
- Throw this pitch with the same arm speed and body mechanics as a fastball, only slightly turn the ball over by throwing the circle to the target. This is called pronating your hand. (Think about this as giving someone standing directly in front of you a "thumbs down" sign with your throwing hand.) This reduces speed and gives you that nice, fading movement to your throwing-arm side of the plate.

KNUCKLEBALL

A knuckleball is a baseball pitch thrown that minimizes the spin of the ball in flight, which in turn causes an unpredictable motion. The air flow over a seam of the ball causes the ball to transition to a more turbulent flow. This turbulent flow adds a deflecting force on the side of the baseball, which makes the pitch difficult to hit. However, it also becomes difficult for pitchers to control, catchers to catch and for umpires to call balls and strikes. Early knuckleball pitchers threw the pitch by holding the ball with their knuckles. Other pitchers later modified the pitch by gripping the ball with fingertips, digging the fingernails into the surface of the ball and using the thumb for balance. The fingertip grip is more commonly used today by knuckleball pitchers.

UMPIRES

For dribblers down the 3rd base or 1 st base line if the ball stays fair it's the home plate umpires call. If the ball passes the bag then it's the 3rd base or 1 st base umpires call.

Pitcher's who welcome rookies to the big league by drilling them in the back should be tossed.

If the catcher calls for and is set up for an inside pitch but must shift across the plate because the pitch hits the outside corner, the pitcher may not get the call from the umpire.

Umpires don't want to see movement from the catcher. If the catcher is set up a couple of inches off the plate and the pitcher is constantly hitting that spot, it's hard for an umpire not to call it.

Umpires should not over-react to a hit batter after a home run. Give a warning. However, a warning is not fair to the opposing team because if the opposing team retaliates, the pitcher and/or manager will be tossed.

Umpires should attempt to speed up the game by standardizing the strike zone, encouraging pitcher's to work quickly, decrease the number times a batter can step out of the batter's box, and limit mound visits by players, coaches and managers. Duration and pace of games are out of sync with fan base who need to go home and go to work and kids who have to go to school.

If an umpire is consistently calling a borderline pitch a strike, the hitter should accept it, stop complaining and made the adjustment.

There should be only one home plate for both teams. A low strike for one team should be a low strike for both teams. Umpires must be consistent.

Umpires should refrain from the delayed strike calls. It's frustrating to the catcher, pitcher and hitter. When you see it, quickly call it.

Managers may test the umpires to a point without getting thrown out just to let them know that they are unhappy with the strike zone.

If a ball bounces in fair territory, then goes over the 3rd base bag in fair territory but then bounces in foul territory, it's a fair ball.

Chapter 14

MISC

If hitters are not putting the ball into play, it's a sign that the pitcher has good stuff.

Turf is a fast field. Natural grass is slow field. Managers and coaches should plan their line-up and defense accordingly.

Sometime it's better to break an ankle then sprain an ankle.

Sometimes a home run can stop a rally.

If a batter swings and miss's and is hit at the same time, the swinging strike supersedes the hit bat's men.

Every team is hunting for righty power

50% of lead off walks score.

Pitcher's who throw across their bodies will most likely not have a long pitching career and are susceptible to arm injuries.

There is no credible data which confirms that by shutting down a pitcher or limiting a pitcher's innings will prevent arm injuries. Not all pitchers need that type of protection. During the 2012 season, Justin Verlander pitched almost 240 inning and was not held to a pitch count as was Stephen Strasburg who posted 159 innings before being shut down for the remainder of the season to include the post-season. Every pitcher is different. Some guys fatigue at 90-100 pitches and some don't. How would you know if you don't let them pitch past that point?

In the wake of the recent arm injury to Met Pitcher Matt Harvey, former Met great Tom Seaver stated that pitchers today are being babied too much. Pitch counts and innings pitch is nonsense to Seaver. Some injuries can't be predicted and there's not a lot you can do to prevent them other then refining your mechanics. Pitchers today should build up and condition their arms by pitching more not less. Seaver went on to name pitchers such as Palmer, Carlton, Jenkins, Marichal and Spahn who constantly threw over 300 innings with no pitch count. Seaver concluded by saying that there is no numerical value you put on a pitchers arm. Pitchers are all different. Instead of treating pitchers like robots and worrying about how many pitches they have left in their arms, they should weight the determination and competitive spirit they have in their minds and heart.

From a physical stand point the arm is not designed to throw a FB 98-100 mph

Pitchers with a perfect delivery and mechanics still develop arm injuries.

In the 50's and 60's rotor cuff and ACL injuries were un-heard of. Since most contracts in those days were 1 year type, most likely pitchers just pitched through their injuries.

In addition to command of their FB, pitchers also require poise and maturity. Some pitchers lose their concentration after giving up a few hits, walks or runs. Pitchers must focus on the next hitter with the mind-set that a ground ball a/o DP will get him out of the inning.

Extra innings go longer because hitters are trying hard to hit home runs instead of piecing together a few hits to score the winning go ahead run.

When playing a bad team you need to get to them early and knock them out of the game as they may pack it in.

The 1st base coach should remind runners how many outs there are.

The 1st base coach should try to determine the pitchers pattern to assist the runners steal attempt.

If the ball is dribbled down the 3rd base line, hits the bag and caroms out to left field, the 1st base coach should be alert and signal the runner to proceed to 2nd base.

Home runs follow walks because the pitch has to get the ball over the plate.

In ball parks where balls carry and out-fielders play deeper, they are also more separate. Thus more hits are possible.

Most short reliever's don't have a good move to 1st base.

A reliever throwing 4 straight balls for an IW may get out of sync with his pitch concentration. Have the pitcher being relieved issue the IW.

If you are not a good 2 strike hitter, you most likely will not hit for average.

Tall lanky pitchers with long arms and come overhead are known as down-hill pitchers. The ball is on top of you quickly.

When facing "Lights Out" pitchers, teams should rely on speed, small ball, patient at balls and team defense.

Some hitters hold the bat down past the bottom nub of the bat. Not certain what advantage this provides other then what a hitter may be comfortable with or has become use to. If he hits for average, it should not be a concern. If not, maybe the hitting coach should intervene. Also, in holding the bat in that manner, you now run the risk of losing the bat with a hard swing. The bat could fly into either dugout of into the stands and injury someone.

In an effort to protect pitchers from line drives, there is talk of providing helmets to pitchers. Don't know if this is a good or bad idea. However, pitchers will continue to be susceptible to serious injury from line drives until they position themselves correctly after delivering a pitch. After pitch delivery, both feet should be even with a slight bend at the waist and both hands up facing home plate. As opposed to falling to the 1st base or 3rd base side of the mound leaving the face and entire body exposed. This is the job of the pitching coach to instill this safety measure. However, most pitching coaches and managers are reluctant to tamper with a pitchers delivery style, especially if he's winning pitcher.

With a slow runner on 3rd and a high chopper, the 3rd base coach should tell the runner to use his best judgment.

Catchers don't catch high sinkers. Hitters will hit high sinkers.

The higher the top, the bigger the drop is a saying for tall pitchers throwing curve balls.

General Manager's need to reconsider giving mega contracts to an individual as opposed to investing the money in two or three other positions.

Player's need to understand that negotiations is business and should not be made personal (i.e. the team did not respect me) It's incumbent upon management to get you signed as cheaply as possible. If you are a star player and the team is not offering what you are demanding, you need to consider if you can make up the difference off the field especially if you are in a big market town. During negotiations you can get creative to do things to make it work) i.e. (defer a certain amount) this way the team stays under the cap and the player gets his money. The bottom line is that negotiations are business driven and management will make their offer based on what they think is right and can afford.

Chapter 15

JAPANESE IMPORTS

When signing pitchers from Japan it should be noted that the mound in MLB is higher and the ball is slightly bigger. Import pitchers may need extra work with the larger ball to see movement on their pitches. Japanese pitchers must also adjust to a five man rotation or pitching an every 5th day rotation as in Japan they only pitch once a week. To that end it will be important for Japanese pitchers to get extra rest in order to keep up their strength through the year. Finally, you may need to import another player from Japan who speaks English to provide support and companionship.

Chapter 16

NEW VIDEO INSTANCE REPLAY

Managers will be allowed one challenge over the first six innings of games and two until the completion of the game as such managers will have to be judicious in their use.

Challenges do not carry over. Its use or lose. If the 1st challenge is not use during the first 6 innings, the manager will only have two remaining for the rest of the game.

If the challenge is not successful, the manager will lose a challenge. If it is successful, he will keep his remaining challenges.

Calls that are challenged will be reviewed by a crew in MLB headquarters in New York City in which will make the final ruling.

What this means is no more temper tantrums by managers. Instead we will have challenge flags

Managers will now have power over close calls involving plays other then the strike zone and umpires will have to be receptive

If a manager runs out of challenges, he would still be able to ask for reviews of questionable homeruns.

Bottom line – everything besides balls and strikes is challengeable and homeruns reviewable

Each manager gets at least one challenge. If he wins the first challenge, he gets a second one, if not, his challenges are gone. After the 6th inning the crew chief can call for his own challenge on a disputed play. All replays will be looked at in MLB's New York Replay Command Center.

Plays that can be challenged: Home run, ground rule double, fan interference, stadium boundary calls, force play, tag play, fair/foul in outfield only, trap play in outfield only, batter hit by pitch, timing play, touching a base, passing runners and record keeping.

At this time it's not certain how this will affect the minor league or preseason games. But for certain we could be staring at 4 hour games.

Chapter 17

NOTABLE SAYINGS

Blind people come to the park just to listen to him pitch. – Reggie Jackson speaking about Tom Seaver

What did he throw me? If I had seen em, I'd have a better way of telling you about em. – Pete Rose speaking about Dwight Gooden

The worst part is after he's done striking out 10 of your guys, he goes and leaps tall buildings with a single bound. – Carl Yastrzemski speaking of Ron Guidry.

Show FB inside but don't try to get them out there – Jim Bunning

Show me a pitcher who lives inside and I will show you a loser. – Sandy Koufax

Pillow contract is a short term deal to reestablish a player's market value. A term allegedly invented by Scott Boras.

Sometimes when a pitcher is in trouble, whether it is his fault or the result of bad defense, he has to take it upon himself to reach for something extra and get out of the jam and pick up his teammates. – Don Drysdale

The pitcher throws the ball, I see the ball, and I hit the ball. – Willie Mays

Player contracts do not read that the team will finish above 500.

PINE TAR

This past season saw several incidents involving pine tar. Rule 8.02(3) states that pitchers shall not apply a foreign substance of any kind to the ball. It may be time to revise that rule and allow pitchers to allow a limited amount of pine tar or some other type of approved substance to assist the pitcher on a cold or wet night. Pitchers are not the only ones who use pine tar, as hitters use it legally and infielders use it on their gloves to help get a better grip on the ball.

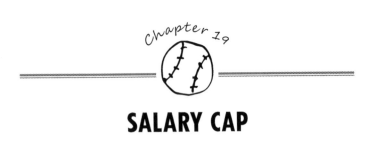

SALARY CAP

All teams must be under the salary cap of $189 million dollars. If not they are penalized with the luxury tax. The $189 million dollar pay roll limitation is for the entire 25 man roster. Each team budgets roughly $5 million dollars for in-season call ups resulting from poor player performance or injuries. In addition, each team is charged roughly $11 million dollars for benefits such as insurance and pensions. The $5 million and $11 million are included in the $189 million dollar cap.

Chapter 20

LUXURY TAX

Technically called the "Competitive Balance Tax", the Luxury Tax is the punishment that large market teams get for spending too much money. While MLB does not have a set salary cap, the luxury tax charges teams with high payrolls a considerable amount of money, giving teams ample reason to want to keep their payrolls below that level.

The luxury tax remained relatively unchanged in the new CBA. The threshold level for the luxury tax will be $178 million in both 2012 and 2013 (the same as it was in 2011), and will be raised to $189 million from 2014-2016. And offenders will be charged the following tax rates, depending on how many years in a row they have been above the threshold:

First time: 17.5%
Second time: 30%
Third time: 40%
Fourth time and higher: 50%

Any team that drops below the threshold will reset their luxury tax rate, dropping them back down to the first time rate (17.5%) if they should happen to go over the threshold again in the future.

Money raised through the luxury tax is set aside for industry development — not revenue sharing, as is commonly thought. It is distributed as such: the first $2.5 million is reserved for potential refunds, and then 75% is given to fund player benefits and 25% goes to the Industry Growth Fund

Chapter 21

HARD HATS FOR PITCHERS

MLB has approved a protective cap for pitchers in an attempt to reduce the damage and injuries suffered from line drives to the head. The new hat was recently introduced and will be available for testing during spring training on a voluntary basis. Major leaguers and minor league players will not be required to wear it. The safety plates made by isoBLOX are sewn into the hat and custom fitted. It will weight an extra 6-7 ounces. It will offer protection to the forehead, temple, and side of the head. It will make the hat about a ½ inch thicker in the front and around an inch wider on the sides. Hopefully this new hat will preclude line drive type injuries will have resulted in brain contusion and skull fracture.

Chapter 22

NEW PLATE BLOCKING
RULES FOR CATCHERS

New rules will soon be passed down from MLB that will
ban home plate collisions. It's not clear exactly when
the rules will be implemented. However, some clubs
are assuming that the rule will be adopted in 2014
or 2015. The league and the Union are working out
the language of the rules. Clubs are instructing their
catchers accordingly to have them prepared to handle
plays consistent with the soon to be implemented rule
change. The new rule basically has the catcher standing
of the edge or border of the plate providing a lane for
the runner to slide thus avoiding a collision. The catcher
will have to reach to make a tag. Bottom line is that
catchers can no longer block the plate. Catcher's must
show the runner the plate and provide him a lane to
slide. Catchers must position themselves in fair territory
with their left foot up against the left side of the plate.
If catchers violate the new rules, there will be penalties.
At this point it's not certain what those penalties with
be or how they would be implemented.

Chapter 23

PITCHER PROTECTION

As pitchers stand only 60 feet and 6 inches from home plate, there has been a string of injuries as a result of line drives off the bat of hitters. Some of the injuries include concussions, broken noses, injury to eye socket, contusions and lacerations. To combat these types of injuries, the league has approved the use of isoBLOX padded caps (they are ugly) that are slightly more than half-inch thicker in the front and an inch thicker near the temples than standard caps. These new caps will provide pitchers frontal impact protection against liners up to speeds of 90 mph and up to 85 mph on the sides. The caps have been made available to all major league teams (not sure about the minors) however, it doesn't appear that they are being worn enmass.

Chapter 24

RULE 5

The **Rule 5 draft** is a <u>Major League Baseball</u> player <u>draft</u> that occurs each year in December, at the annual <u>Winter Meeting of general managers</u>. The Rule 5 draft aims to prevent teams from stockpiling too many young players on their <u>minor league</u> affiliate teams when other teams would be willing to have them play in the majors.[1] The Rule 5 draft is named for its place in Major League Rules. The June <u>Rule 4 draft</u>, known as simply "the draft", "amateur draft", or "first year player draft", is a distinctly different process in which team's select high school and college players.

Chapter 25

NEW RULES

Hitters will be required to keep at least one foot in the batter's box.

Clocks will be installed on or near outfield scoreboards and on facades behind home plate. Inning breaks will be counted down from 2:25 for locally televised games and 2:45 for nationally televised games. Pitchers must throw their last warm-up pitch before 30 seconds is remaining. The only exception is when the pitcher or catcher is on base when the previous ½ innings ends. Fines for violations will be capped at $500.00

Managers will no longer have to leave their dugouts to call for replays unless the play in question ends an inning and the defensive team must be kept on the field.

For the first time, plays involving whether a runner left a base early or touched a base on a tag up play will be subject to a video review.

Managers will retain the challenge for every overturned call not just the first. Managers will also have two

Lenzy Kelley Jr.

challenges during tiebreaker, postseason and all-star games.

The manager will be required to use challenge to review violations of the home plate collision rule.

The crew chief may call for a review from the 7th inning on if a manager is out of challenges.

There is no longer a 20 second clock between pitches.

There is no longer a limit to pitcher mount visits involving catchers and managers.

The above cited items are intended to speed up the pace of the game. While well intended, it does not address TV commercials and managers who over manage. A 5-3 game could very well see 8-10 pitchers. An untouchable reliever in the 8th inning is removed for a 9th inning closer.

Chapter 26

LEGEND

BP – Baseball

FB – Fastball

SZ – Strike Zone

DP – Double Play

SS – Short Stop

BM – Baseman

LHH – Left hand hitter

RHH – Right hand hitter

LFP – Left hand Pitcher

RHP – Right hand Pitcher

IW – Intentional Walk

IR – Injured Reserve

CREDITS

Daily News Interview with Met Pitcher Tom Glavine, 16 Feb 2003.

New York Post, Sound Off, 14 June 2009

New York Post Article by Dan Martin Re: R.A. Dickey, 20 June 2012

New York Post "Sound Off" Article, 5 August 2012

New York Post Article by Joel Sherman, 13 October 2012

New York Post Article by Ken Davidoff, 29 October 2012

New York Post article by Mike Puma, dated 16 April 2013.

New York Post article by Mike Puma, dated 24 April 2013

New York Daily News Sports Wire article, dated 26 April 2013

New York Daily news article by John Harper, dated 30 April 2013

The Complete Pitcher.Com by Steven Ellis

New York Daily news article by Bill Madden, dated 19 May 2013

New York Post article by Zach Braziller dated 1 July 2013.

Lenzy Kelley Jr.

New York Post article by Mark Hale, dated 5 July 2013

New York Daily news articles by Bill Madden and John Harper dated 16 August 2013.

New York Post article by Jonathan Lehman dated 17 August 2013.

New York Daily news article by Bill Madden dated 30 August 2013.

New York Daily News article by John Harper dated 1 September 2013.

New York Post Article by Joel Sherman, dated 18 January 2014

Biz of Baseball via Google

New York Daily news article by Andy Martino, dated 18 February 2014

New York Daily news article by Mark Feinsand, dated 22 Feb 2014

New York Daily news article by Andy Martino, dated 16 March 2014

New York Daily news article by Andy Martino dated 21 June 2014.

New York Magazine article, The Glass Arm by Will Leitch, dated March 2013

From Wikipedia, the free encyclopedia (TJS)

New York Daily News article by Bill Madden dated 6 April 2014.

New York Daily News article by Andy Martino, dated 12 April 2014

New York Post article by George A. King III, dated 12 April 2014

New York Daily News article by John Harper, dated 11 June 2014

New York Post article by George A. King III, dated 11 June 2014

New York Daily News article by Wayne Coffey dated 13 July 2014

New York Post article by Joel Sherman dated 30 September 2014

New York Post article by Joel Sherman, dated 9 October 2014

New York Post article by Joel Sherman dated 12 October 2014.

New York Post article by Joel Sherman dated 21 February 2015.

New York Post article by Joel Sherman dated 15 March 2015.

New York Post article by Kevin Kerman dated 16 March 2015.

New York Daily News "Voice of the People articles by Roland Dattner and Greg Rohaus dated 23 March 2015.

New York Post article by Mike Vaccaro dated 25 March 2015.

Asbury Park Press article by Chad Jennings, dated 22 April 2015

From Wikipedia, the free encyclopedia (R5)